Greater Day Greater Sun

MEKESHA LEONIE SHEPHERD

Tellwell Talent
www.tellwell.ca

ISBN
978-0-2288-6372-4 (Paperback)
978-0-2288-6373-1 (eBook)

TABLE OF CONTENTS

CHAPTER 1

The Circles of Life

Come to paradise it will make you feel all right. Come to paradise and everything will be nice; all your troubles and worries will be over. Those are a few people's thoughts and perceptions about where I'm from—especially from people living abroad, looking from the outside in, as opposed to those who are living there, looking in.

I was born to my mother, Lee, and father, George. There came a time in their lives when they decided to have children together and I was one of them. They decided to name me Mekesha Leonie. That is the name I was born and raised with. Further on in life my family and close friends started calling me Bluff! My uncles gave me that alias. It was a common practice to have a pet name in the family. But for the life of me, I just could not understand or begin to comprehend why that alias has stuck to me like glue, ever since.

I was born and raised on the small island of Jamaica, just off the coast, east of the Caribbean Sea. My mother gave birth to me in May at the Victoria Jubilee Hospital. Unless you lived in some remote village, far along the countryside, then that hospital in downtown Kingston is where you were born. I grew up in Rock fort, Kingston, Jamaica, until I was eleven years old. That is not too far from the famous Michael Norman Manley International Airport.

To many people, Rock fort was regarded as a very rough and tough neighbourhood. It was typically identified as the ghetto and I couldn't agree more. It was a poverty-stricken, violent, dangerous, and oppressive place to live. At the same time, there were a lot of decent, hardworking people living there too. I was taught by my parents how to live and co-exist with others no matter where you live or where you come from. You kind of get used to that sort of place. After a while my body and mind became immune to my surroundings. After all, every ghetto has its times and seasons for violence, full throttle, and its moments for fun, enjoyment, and pleasures. Over the years, I managed to adjust by learning how to adapt and take the good with the bad.

I lived in a small house with my parents, three older sisters, and two brothers. My mother had a total of six children: four with my father and two from a previous relationship before I was born. My three older sisters were Angelica, Royal, and Andrea. I had two brothers by the names of Audley and Ian. Audley was my mother's first-born son. He and my sister Royal weren't my father's biological children; nevertheless, my father loved and treated them just the same as the rest of us. My mother had my older brother at a young age and met my father a few years thereafter. Then there was Ian. He was the youngest of my mother's children. He was also the one and only biological son of my father. After my younger brother was born my mother decided to have tubal ligation surgery done, so she couldn't produce any more children. She said six was more than enough for her and it was time for her to hang up those boots. I couldn't agree with her more from that perspective.

My brother Ian was considered the baby of the family, naturally. I was the fifth child, and he was the sixth, so we were close to each other in age. We had a different kind of bond from the rest of my siblings. My younger brother and I were close because we were both the youngest and were only two years apart in age. Those aren't uncommon reasons for siblings to be close in other families either.

Perhaps we are also close because we both had that competitive spirit and drive with just a bit of fire in the belly in everything that we did. We would always push each other to do the best we could in anything and to strive for the best, whether it was in athletics or academics or anything else for that matter. He displayed great respect for me and that was gratifying for me—to know that I was doing my job and my sisterly duties.

We lived in a five-bedroom house, but technically my family had control of three out of the five rooms, so there was less than fifty percent of the whole house for me to play the proper role of being a big sister to him and a damn good one for sure. He wasn't just a little brother to me either; he was also my best friend. People would often mistakenly take us for twins and that was all right with me. I knew that my brother valued the entire house. The reason for that was that the other two rooms were occupied by two separate tenants by the names of Buzz and Baps. Buzz lived in the room around the back of the yard as a single bachelor. Baps lived in the other room located at the front of the house with her daughter Sharon. The mother and daughter seemed to argue with each other every chance that they got. Their arguments became hard to ignore considering their room was facing mine in the middle of the hallway passage right next to the verandah.

My mom and dad occupied the other front room on the opposite side of the verandah. My brother Audley stayed in the back room, where he enjoyed peace and quiet to himself. He also made it a regular habit to bring in different girlfriends from the neighbourhood on a regular basis to have rendezvous with, whether it was night or day. He didn't even claim most of them to be his girlfriend. He would just use them to have a good time . . . sort of like a wham, bam, thank you, ma'am, sort of thing. I found his action to be a bit appalling, with no regard for others, poor girls, but I'm pretty sure that some of them knew exactly what they were getting up to. At the same time, some of the girls that came over should have been taught how to keep the lid closed on the cookie jar. There was no shame in either of their games!

Audley was very adamant about anyone going inside his room; he didn't like anyone of his siblings entering his room except for Angelica. The frown on his face and his body language alone spoke loud and clear. Perhaps the reasons why he allowed Angelica to enter his room were because they were close in age with just a few years difference. I mean they were best friends and very tight knit. They knew and kept each other's secrets. They told each other everything.

There were times that the rest of us were cramped in like sardines in a tin. All five of us were in a room while Audley had a full room to himself. I just couldn't really comprehend the logical reasoning for his selfishness. We were a big family and there wasn't that much space and rooms for the rest of us to go in that house except for outside.

Audley at times would take the liberty to make fun of me and the rest of my siblings, except for Angelica of course; she was his favourite sister without a doubt. Audley would often make fun of me and the rest of my siblings at times, whether it was the kink in my hair or whether he was giving me a candid description of how big my nose was, he just couldn't help putting others down. What truly annoyed me was when he would constantly invade my space and peace of mind by literally squeezing my nose every chance he got and constantly reminding me of how big it was. He would also take aim at the way that I was dressed every chance that he got. He would just go ham on us more for no apparent reason. Maybe it made him feel better about himself. He would often hurt my feelings and make me feel inadequate about myself. The rest of my siblings would often complain to each other about his irrational behaviour but not to his face.

Perhaps if we had had the courage and guts to tell him about our true feelings of how he had really bullied and ridiculed us over the years he would have knocked it off . . . or maybe not. On the other hand, I don't think it would have made much difference to him at all. I'm pretty sure he would have made fun of our opinions as usual. He has never taken accountability for anything! I strongly get the impression from him that he somehow felt he was superior to the rest of us. Maybe it was because my mother petted him like an egg, or he was her prize petunia or something. I mean, I don't mean to sound harsh, but to be frank, he was hard deal with at times.

I came to know him as Audley the asshole, and I also knew that he was my eldest brother. I had to live with him, love him, and accept who he was because he wasn't going to change anytime soon to suit any of us that had a problem with him. Even though he was quite mean and arrogant with no apology, I had to learn how to forgive him at times for his foolery, and I was still proud at times and glad that he was my big brother. There is an old saying that goes, "Seven children, seven different minds." In this case, it was six children. We are not all made the same or function the same.

My father, George, was a carpenter and my mother, Lee, was a nurse. We were never rich, but to my knowledge, we had a decent life. We had our moments where we had to scrimp on food now and then. We would sometimes eat a lot of mackerels and sardines to get us through the week until payday came for my parents. Those canned goods were cheaper to purchase, but they sure tasted good in times of hunger. We had a lot of pride, so we made it our priority not to tell anyone when we were breaking and struggling. No one knew but us when we weren't financially able to take care of the necessities within our household; we had to learn how to bear our wants and needs. It wasn't something that we would want to share with anyone that we were running short on money and food or anything else for that matter. Besides, we were only taking precautionary measures by not telling anyone when we were breaking. We were fearful that it would end up on the front-page news of the daily Gleaner or perhaps be broadcasted on the air. People gossiped a lot about each other and other people's business, especially the people in my neighbourhood. Some of them were far worse off than we were but that didn't seem to stop them from gossiping about other people's lives. I got the feeling and the sense that my family had a lot of pride, and my parents wore their hearts on their sleeves. They were well respected by other people anyway. Maybe it was because both of my parents had decent jobs, so we were perceived as having a bit more. But little did others know that we had to struggle like everyone one else, and we had a big family apparently with a lot of mouths to feed.

Some people thought we had everything mainly because of the way we carried ourselves. We didn't act like unreasonable vulgar hooligans; it was important to stay focused and grounded by having proper manners and showing respect to others, especially our elders. We were also taught by our parents how to be empathic. We were not living for ourselves alone, for one man cannot live on an island alone either. We were rational, reasonable people to my knowledge, or at least I would like to think that we were.

We wore clean clothes and some of us wore proper shoes on our feet, sometimes but not all the time. My mother tried, and she didn't always get it right. There was no money pit hidden. There were some shoes, clothing, and certain items that you loved so much, because every time you wore them, they made you feel good, so you didn't want to part with them. After a while, those items would get burned out and pop down and start to lose their colour and texture. I mean our hair was nicely groomed—well most of the time—but as for me, the struggles were real when it came to my mother and sisters combing my hair. My hair was hard to deal with because there was just something about the kinks and *kaya* in my hair. My mother always had to use a hot-pressing comb in my hair, and she had to fight hard to find me a suitable hairstyle week in and week out.

Thanks to George and Lee for making sure that we had a decent home, a decent life and nice things. We were fortunate to have a television and to get the latest dolls or action figures, like G.I. Joe, He-Man, and Transformers, for my little brother and so on. We felt loved, special and appreciated by our family no matter what the situation or circumstance. Maybe as far back as I can remember, George and Lee always encouraged us to work hard in everything, play fair, and try to do our best to obtain and achieve our goals because they said the universe is a never-ending place and that life does not stop in one place. But most of all they taught us that to be honest and kind and to respect ourselves was mandatory. We learned that proper manners go a long way in this world.

I and my two brothers and three sisters were constantly told by our parents to be careful in our comings and goings as we would stroll sometimes through some of the toughest and roughest streets to go about our business in Kingston. Places like Nanny Ville, Jarret Lane, Mountain View, Warwick, Gully, and Commission Road were just a few hot spots that dealt with badness.

Some of my most memorable moments growing up were visiting my uncle Evan and the cousins from my mother's side of the family that lived on Commission Road. My sisters and I made it our priority to visit my uncle as much as we could during the weekends. Uncle Evan was a shoemaker and a good one at that, he was a great uncle and great role model that I looked up to. Whenever we would visit him, he always made me and my siblings feel welcome and treated us how he would treat his children. He was a great person and one of the best uncles I ever had.

There were often other reasons and circumstances that led us to certain neighbourhoods: visiting our dressmakers that made our school uniforms or just visiting a friend from school or dance classes. Growing up I had no choice but to walk through a certain neighbourhood and area. We learned firsthand that it was best to stay out of certain communities and environments as much as we could because there were always a few gunmen that might be hitched up on the street corners looking out for strange faces in their neighbourhood one way or another. Even when we didn't see them or even know who they were, they managed to see us coming from far and near. They just had an eye and a neck for strange faces.

If we could avoid certain areas, it was best that we did so as much as possible. But it is so hard at times to do so because some of our closest friends and family lived in many of those garrisons. Nevertheless, if we happened to be there for some reason or passed through or stumbled upon one of those bad neighborhoods like mine, we did so at your own risk and proceeded with caution. We would go about our business swiftly and safely. We might have stood a better chance during the day, but in the evening or night hours we wouldn't want to be caught in certain places because we just didn't want any smoke or to get smoked, figuratively speaking. Some neighbourhoods had bigger guns and more ammunition than what was used in the Gulf War. I could never understand where the poor got money from to supply their dirty habits and fuel their wicked ways.

In most neighbourhoods like mine if people happened to see or witness certain actions others might find disagreeable, it was just better sometimes to turn a blind eye or a deaf ear. That did not make anyone a coward, The truth is that no one wanted any drama or the possibility of losing their life or wanting any involvement with the police and being labelled by others as an informer. Getting involved with other people's affairs or being an informer did not resonate well at all with others, especially in poor communities. Informers usually stuck out like a sore thumb after a while and they usually ended up somewhere dead, one way or another.

That is truly sad, but that was just the way it was in the ghetto or garrison, whichever name for them you chose. Not to be stereotypical in any shape or manner, but one thing that I know for sure is that people that lived in the ghetto had a lot of personal issues, whether that was stress, poverty, or mental health, just to name a few. One thing that I know for sure is that there were people with more problems than what Dear John read about. Everybody had a story or two and some sort of experience that they had to live through, whether they were rich or poor.

CHAPTER 2

A Small Dose of Reality

In the 1980s my father, George, sat down with the family one day and told us that he had some important news to share with us. He then turned to us and said that he would be leaving us the following week. He had received a telegram from Immigration stating that everything was in order, and he been granted a temporary visa to go and visit his cousins abroad in Canada. Apparently, his cousins had sent him an invitation letter many months prior, requesting my father come and visit them. Without hesitation, George decided to take his cousins up on their offer.

My father also told us that his cousins had purchased a plane ticket for him, so that was really a bonus that he didn't have to do that. If he had had to purchase that pricey plane ticket, we would have been distressed. I don't know how my father and mother would have managed. Such an expense would have surely boxed bread off the table for us, and we wouldn't have been able to eat properly and pay our expenses for months. It is really a crime within itself, to be poor.

My father had a very close relationship with his two first cousins, Danny and Bunny. He grew up with them in the parish of Portland, Orange Bay, from when he was a young boy to an adult. George's father and his cousins' fathers were brothers. Even though my father had four brothers of his own, his cousins were also like his brothers and truly near and dear to him. I was ecstatic for my father, and really, he deserved a break and every bit of success. He must have had the best cousins in the whole world. My father's cousins were like his brother's keeper. Ever since they were youths, those two brothers, Bunny and that good old Danny old boy, were always looking out for him. They remained selfless when it came to helping my father, and for that, I will forever be grateful to them.

That my father had an opportunity to travel and visit a foreign land was such exciting and major news for me and the rest of my family, for his success was our success as well. No one in our family had taken a plane before to travel abroad, except for my grandmothers. They both lived in England at the time, at least the last time I heard. They both have been missing in action since way before I was even born. Talk about dysfunction junction. I wondered many times if they even existed or were only a myth. Neither of them played that Granny role that we so desperately needed. At the time they were not seen nor heard from by my parents. I suppose they were so caught up in their lifestyles in England to say hello from the other side. I often wonder to myself if they just cared enough that things might have somehow been different.

I was learning the ropes and important aspects of family at an early age, but the truth of the matter was that life was forcing me to grow up quicker than I could've even anticipated. Even though I still didn't fully understand some things or fully grasp what was happening around me, life in Jamaica was a steppingstone, and I was stepping and learning along the way.

Naturally, my imagination would sometimes take me on a journey into La-La land. I would imagine myself flying in a big plane travelling halfway around the world, living the life and the dream. Oh, the possibilities for me were endless. My perception of "foreign" was that it was the land of milk and honey and where dreams were made of. It was a world filled with a lot of glitz and glamour where people wore fancy clothing and attended their fancy parties, sort of like those old Hollywood movies, glam and lifestyle. Oh me, oh my, the imagination is a wonderful thing to have. It is always a way to escape reality.

I often buried my feelings in my imagination because it was easier to do so. I desired to have a great life of peace and stillness, where I could walk around from place to place, freely, and not have to look over my shoulders. I wanted a life where I didn't have to worry about the violence and the bloodshed of everyday life and the people that surrounded me. To me, "foreign" was a ticket to get out of the Ghetto and have a better life far away from the struggles of physical and mental oppression that I saw people suffer daily and away from the people there as well. I just wanted to be in a haven where I could run about freely to express myself and ideas without second-guessing myself. Besides that, who wouldn't want to eat all the ice cream, cotton candy, candy apples and other delicious treats that were waiting abroad?

As the weeks, days and time passed by I had so many mixed feelings and emotions. One day I was happy and running about and another time I was feeling sad and everything that was around me seemed dry and dull, especially in my household. The atmosphere within my household felt bleak and at times lonely. I began to feel a little uneasy and emotionally unstable. That feeling was something completely new for me. I can't ever in my young life recall feeling that way. Perhaps I was just going through the motions and feeling a sense of abandonment that my father had to leave us soon. I had always had that codependency with both parents around me all my life. I relied on my parents for everything and the idea of not having one of them around began to weigh heavily on me.

Everything was happening so fast and started to manifest and spilled over into my world. I would often wonder what it would be like once my father was gone, my ever so kind and loving father, who had helped my mother raise me from birth. I had admired, respected and loved him throughout my entire life. He was always a trying and selfless man, always putting his family first. I was truly fortunate to have him as my father.

I somehow felt the changing of the guards. Things were moving and changing more quickly than I had anticipated, and I knew things were not going to get any easier for us, down the road from then on out and soon. The question remained for me as to who was going to be that person in the family to step up to the plate and take care of the family whenever my mother wasn't around. Who was going to be there to sing me folk songs and read to me and tell me Anansi stories? Who was going to be the one who emerged to be that extra shoulder to lean and cry on? Who was going to be the one to help me say my prayer at night and teach me how to sing them old folk songs? I had a lot of unanswered questions that were raising some concerns and were worrisome for me at a young age.

The one thing that I knew for sure was it was all up to Mama from then on to do what needed to be done to hold down the fort. What a heavy load for my mother to bear on her own from there on out and especially in the ghetto where she was among pretenders and was surrounded by a bunch of hypocritical, mischievous people that were like some crabs in a bucket that were always up to no good.

It was a Tuesday afternoon, and my father was scheduled to leave on that Thursday morning. His time was near, and the moment of truth was close. I didn't think that I was ready and fully prepared as a youngling for my father to leave me to go away yet, but the choice was not mine. At the same time, my father had to do what he needed to do in search of a better life. He wanted a way out of the Ghetto once and for all. After all, opportunity comes but once sometimes. He clearly understood what was at stake and was willing to take his chances. No risk, no reward. No pain, no gain!

The next day my mother helped my father pack the rest of his belongings and double-check his suitcases to see if he had everything that he needed. My mother helped him to tuck away his belongings nice and neat for the long journey that was ahead of him. He was also taking precautionary measures because there were uncertainties as to how long he was staying abroad. At the same time, he wasn't planning on taking much with him. He was only taking the basics necessities and a few going out clothes and casual clothing just in case he found a job abroad. He just wanted to prepare himself for his first visit to the foreign lands in Canada.

After all, it was not like he was going abroad forever to live; he solemnly took an oath and had assured our family with confidence that he was coming back soon. He was only going to visit relatives and to find a job that paid under the table so he could use it. So, he didn't need to take all his clothing and the rest of his belongings with him to Canada, I'm just saying. The more my mother helped my father pack, the more depressed and sulkier she began to look. Her body language and face spoke to me louder than words. I suppose most of us were feeling that way. After all, we were just flesh and blood with feelings and emotions . . . maybe too much at times.

But, of course, Lee tried to take it all in stride because that was the type of woman that she was. She would always put on a brave face and support the family. She pretended as if everything was just dandy, even in moments when they were not. She understood that it was a memorable occasion for my father and the rest of the family. It was bittersweet for us all and I knew in time that it was going to be all right. I had to trust and believe that everything would work itself out.

I had a happy household for the most part. My parents were always polite, loving, and very cordial to each, at least that is what I'd seen. My parents had respect for each other at the time and others admired their strengths too and took care of each other. Besides, why wouldn't my father miss my mother dearly? They were soul mates. They were made for each other, and they were very much in love with each other. She was about five feet two inches tall, medium built, with a beautiful bronze complexion and a lovely oval-shaped face with an impeccable bone structure. Her eyes were small and looked almost

Asian. She still had a small waist and hourglass figure after having all those children. She also had some nice, toned legs and her skin was as smooth as butter. Other women didn't stack up and compare to my mother. My mother was all the woman that my father needed. She was the epitome of wifely material and a very attractive woman.

My father was five feet eleven inches tall, with broad shoulders, a strong build, and good hair. He looked as if he had stepped out of a magazine. To some, he was a chick magnet and the ladies in our community couldn't take their eyes off him, especially because he was always swagged out and very family oriented.

Whenever I went out with my father, women would take the opportunity and the liberty to flirt with him every chance they got. He would constantly remind them that he was already taken, that he was in a relationship with my mother, and that he was very happy and quite content. That is the way it was in the garrison or anywhere else for that matter. Women always want what they can't have and will stop at nothing to satisfy their thirst and cravings, almost like pregnant women. They will not stop until they get what they want!

George and Lee were always kind and caring to each other. When I think about it, I can't ever recall them arguing. They seemed to get along with each other well. From what I understand, they made life for us as peaceful and pleasant as possible. And if they ever did have an argument or made a fuss, it was never put on display for anyone to see. That must have been the best-kept secret for them in this lifetime in that garrison, and trust me, nothing stays secret in those places.

Even though I lived in a violent place, I never experienced any sort of negative emotions or energy with my parents towards each other. Under those circumstances, it was not where you lived but how you lived. People just needed to be smart and have self-awareness and lots of love in their hearts for others. For love conquers all.

To my recollection, my household was a place that was filled with peace and tranquillity between my mom and dad. My home was not filled with hooligans and war mongers, even though I had to take on a rough and tough alter ego when it was needed in the streets. Even though the garrison wasn't an ideal place to live, I had to have some grit or else people would punk me off and then take advantage of me and do me harm. I had to be feisty at times too or else people would curse me out like a dog. I would always pray day and night for the good Lord to give me guidance and a safe passage for me and my family. I would also ask the Lord to especially keep us away from evil doers and people who were set to harm others and to keep violence and bad thoughts from my head.

Cock-a-doodle the cock crowed loudly the next morning. I could never get used to those loud cocks in the mornings. They were such noisy birds. I woke up feeling a bit nostalgic that morning. Perhaps it was because the day had finally come upon us for George to catch his flight to Canada that morning at eight fifteen. It felt like a game of sudden death. So, I got up out of bed, brushed my teeth, washed my face, and did my usual daily routine before going to school.

Then we all sat around the breakfast table, and I remember my father telling us how much he loved us and that we should be good to each other and take good care of ourselves and our mother until he returned. He also told us to stay out of trouble and be safe and to try to do our best in school. He also mentioned again to us to take good care of our mother and that he would write to us soon, every chance he got. He told us not to worry about anything and that he would return as soon as he could. We also told him that we loved him and for him to take care of himself too and that we would miss him greatly. Naturally, as a small child, I never doubted my father's words. Everything that he had said to me up to that point in my life remained true.

He started getting ready shortly after, and when he had finished grooming his taxi arrived to pick him up. We hugged our father and said our final goodbye. I clearly remember waving at him from a distance, from the verandah, as he was heading into the taxi. Then his taxi drove off and there he went into the daylight to the airport.

After my father left, I felt a bit sad, tense, and alone. It was a very trying and emotional time for us all; it felt as if someone had just died and there was a funeral of some sort. Even though I had not been to a funeral, it sure felt like it.

Despite my father's departure, my mother always tried to keep her good spirits up. She remained strong, positive, optimistic, and held down the fort. Unknowns and uncertainties in life never seemed to bother or faze her. She just went about her business as usual, and she made sure that her children did the same. She was undeniably unbreakable. That is why she reigned supreme as my mother, my hero, and my superwoman.

A few days later, the news about my father spread like a California wildfire to other people all over the area. Inquiring minds wanted to know the whereabouts of my father and with vivid details, especially Miss Nosy June. Miss June was the cigarette and candy lady. That was her occupation apart from getting into other people's affairs that is. Every day she would get up bright and early to sit by the roadside in front of her home and sell her products at a cardboard box stall. She made it her priority to see everyone's comings and goings with whom they were coming and going, I must say. She made it her life's work to act as if she was the village lawyer. She resided across the street from me. How unfortunate for us to live across from her. It was pretty annoying as well because she wasn't as sweet as the candy, she was selling either.

Miss June was never my favourite cup of tea; she was a motormouth gossip queen. One day my uncle Garth sent me to buy two packs of Craven A cigarettes from Miss June. In the Caribbean you didn't have to be a certain age to purchase cigarettes, so I put on my slippers with some hesitancy, and I went to her cardboard stall. As

I approached her, she wanted to know the who, the when, the how, and the why: the whole thing about my father's business and him going away to a foreign land. My reply to all her questions was "I don't know." I was hoping that it would keep her interrogation session short. Then she went as far as saying that he was never coming back. How presumptuous and out of order for Miss June to say that I thought. How would she know that? Besides, that's the last thing I wanted to hear. Miss June always had an opinion about other people's business while her business was always spoiling. I guess that was what village lawyers do best; just don't let them see you doing anything.

I couldn't wait for my mother to come home that night so I could tell her about what Miss June had asked and said to me. I was indeed offended by her inquisitive behaviour and lack of moral judgment. When my mother returned home that night, I told her word for word what Miss June had said to me. My mother wasn't surprised, and she took the news rather well. It was not the reaction I had expected. She reacted in a way that was not hyped up. She was clearly unbothered.

She then turned to me with a bit of advice, saying, "You know, Bluff, some people always remain irrelevant, grudge-filled, and full of envy." She also said to me that people were free to say just about anything that they wanted to say—sticks and stones. And that people's motormouths were turned crosswise for a reason—to talk—but that you couldn't let people get you down or get the best of you. My mother was right, and the point was well taken! I guess in a way she was teaching me one of the lessons about having thick skin. A lesson indeed!

What I learned living in the ghetto was you had to have thick skin, and if don't you better grow some, and a backbone while you are at it, to deal with some people. If there are always people gossiping and making inquiries about other people's business, there is just no way of getting away from and around it. People act as if they know more about your business than you do. I suppose it's like that anywhere you go in the world; but in the ghetto, or anywhere else for that matter, that is where their priority lies, so they will never stop. The reality of it all is human nature . . . just saying.

There are also others that don't want other people to elevate themselves or strive be the best that they can be in life. Why? Because they are afraid that others may very well reach their full potential and be further off than them in life. So, their mentality becomes contaminated with negativity. They become bad-minded and have ill intent for others without just cause! Yeah, there were a lot of crabs in a bucket in the garrison for sure, while others waited for you to make a mistake so that they could pounce and put your head on a platter with all pleasure. Some people love to gloat and relish in other people's misery, believe it or not. You know what they say . . . that misery loves company.

In Rock fort, people tried to find ways to lurk about, watching and waiting in the midst for any opportunity to take you down, spreading reckless rumours and gossip about one another, It was unfortunate, but that was just the way it was. People were not there were waiting around to pat you on your shoulders or congratulate you on anything. They were not there to hold your hands and tell you how great you are. Some people have a shady way of thinking with a deep-rooted selfish mentality as if it's every man for himself.

People always wanted to know everything about our family situation—the who, what, when, where, and why—especially about my father being abroad for a long time and how my mother was managing with so many kids and mouths to feed. They would often speculate if she had a new boyfriend yet. Most of them were never truly concerned about us. They wanted to see us go through failures and adversities. They especially wanted to know how my daddy's pocket was, and if he was sending us any monetary funds on a regular basis, or even a jumbo barrel with things, or any parcel. It all came back to wanting to know our business, whether it was good or bad, and they would take it and run with it. People needed to just let it go.

From early on in life I learned not to be too trusting of some people and not to tell others about our family matters. That was just the way it was. People are not always trustworthy and are not always what they seem to appear to be either. They can be messy at times, so it is important that we take precautionary measures about what we utter. Growing up I saw my mother and father get burned by people one too many times. Once you start to let your guard down and you make a mistake and tell them anything, they will act as if you are obliging them on a need-to-know basis. It was my duty to always take precautionary measures, perhaps which is why a part of me has trust issues with others at times. I'm loyal until you cross me, and when you do, there is no turning back.

The truth of the matter is when my father went away abroad for many months, he made a lot of changes in his new life. He wasn't communicating with my mother as much or with any of his children for that matter. The communication barrier between he and his family slowed down immensely over a two-year span. There were days when my father stopped calling as much and my mother stopped receiving letters, telegrams or any monetary funds from my father for months at a time.

After a while, it wasn't all hunky-dory with my parents. My mother began to struggle with her six children for a time and still tried to keep the family afloat. It was hard but she did her best to keep her family's head above water. She always found a way to support us and made sure that we were eating well and still wearing decent clothing. So, people couldn't study us at all. Anyhow, I am pretty sure that some people had their perception of us, but we didn't care. We were bred strong enough to handle whatever obstacle that may come our way. We knew we had each other, and that was all that mattered. We also continued hoping and praying that everything was all right with my father and that the good Lord was keeping him safe.

Lee taught us some simple rules at a young age. Rule One: Do not take food or eat from others under any circumstances because you don't know what is inside the food that might cause harm or poison the body. Rule Two: Do not gossip on the roadside or tell lies and hold conference calls because it usually leads to contention and causes mix-ups. Rule Three: Do not borrow anything whatsoever from people, whether clothing, shoes, or whatever it may be. It was all about having some pride, moral ethics, and standards that we held ourselves to by learning to hold our own. Call it superstition, but in the Caribbean, there is a saying that you don't want to pick up anybody's crosses or bad *juju* (bad luck or bad energy). Rule Four: Always tell your family where you are going or where you are always. If you live by that rule, you should be a okay.

Sometimes people wanted to borrow some of our belongings, and we usually permitted them to, depending on if they were close friends or relatives. Perhaps it was a bit of superstition added to the mix. The bottom line was people were very hard to trust. Even people and close friends in our social circle who pretended to be so trustworthy and pretended to be our close friends tried stealing from us. For instance, I can clearly remember an incident with my oldest sister, Angelica, and close friend Sophia. Sophia came to the residence one weekend and spent the day with my sisters and the rest of us. We laughed, talked, ate and played cards with her that weekend. My family was always delighted to see Sophia and be in her company whenever she came over because she was one of my sister's dearest friends. We had all known for years and always had a good time with her. She was almost like family to us because she was in the dance squad that I and my sisters were in at school. So, she and my sister bonded for years and shared similar experiences in life.

However, Sophia decided to leave our home one evening around a quarter past seven, and as she was leaving the house my sister noticed that she was leaving with a black plastic bag in her hand. So, my sister naturally began questioning me, Royal, and Andrea about the black plastic that Sophia was holding in her hands. Angelica wanted to know if Sophia had had that black plastic bag with her when she arrived at our home. Angelica also used discretion with her line of questioning. She was just making sure that Sophia had brought that bag with her when she came to the house before she went on the attack in a confrontational mood.

Sophia's surprising exit seemed a bit sudden, anxious, and odd to Angelica, so as Sophia began to leave the yard with one foot in and one foot out the gate and the little black plastic bag in her hand, Angelica decided to approach her swiftly and ask her what was inside the bag she was holding. Sophia replied that it was nothing of importance. Well, her answer did not resonate well with Angelica. My sister was not satisfied at all with that response and was determined to prove otherwise. Sophia began to latch on to the plastic bag tightly, as if she was hanging on for dear life. Angelica decided at the moment to make a big grab for the plastic bag and snuck it right out of her hand. The look on Sophia's face was one of pure shock.

Angelica opened the bag and what she saw inside it was alarming. It was a pair of her black ankle cut boots, sandwiched between two baking pans which were used for baking potato pudding. My father had sent those boots for my sister in a small parcel from Canada many months prior. The look on Sophia's face seemed a bit disparaging and I could tell that she was quite embarrassed about the event that had transpired. The rest of us were just standing there with a look of despair and disbelief. We couldn't believe that Sofia of all people would steal from Angelica. Who would have thought that Sophia would do something like that? Who is to say that she hadn't done it before? Who knows! Frankly, I too was a bit embarrassed for heaven's sake. What was she thinking by doing something so repulsive?

I thought that was such a bonehead move on Sophia's part and no one expected that from her. Angelica treated her like a sister and so did the rest of us. She had completely earned our trust. All she had to do was ask for the boots, she didn't have to go that far. I'm pretty sure my sister would have let her borrow those boots of hers. Sophia never had to go to such great lengths to steal from Angelica. Sophia made sure that she apologized to Angelica and the whole nine yards. From where I was standing, she was apologetic and seemed remorseful.

Angelica graciously accepted her apology. She understood that sometimes people make mistakes, especially the ones that we love and care about. People are not perfect, and we have to find it inside of our hearts to forgive them.

My sister forgave Sophia, but I don't think that she ever fully recovered from that incident, no matter how hard she tried. To be honest, their friendship was never on the same level no matter how hard Angelica tried. We would see her all the time almost every day at school. After all, we were on the same dance squad with her, so it would be hard to avoid her. My sister remained cordial with her, and I tried my best to do the same thing. We didn't try to make her feel uncomfortable, or like there was a big pink elephant in the room. If there is one thing that I know for sure, it is that ghetto people didn't like thieves or murderers. They just didn't appreciate that type of behaviour at all, but they could be hypocritical, quite contradictory and contriving at times.

In a sense, in the ghetto people loved to live in happiness, peace, and joy. They liked to enjoy themselves and party and listen to good music to relieve the pressures of stress, poverty, and oppression. Poverty and circumstances made people what they were, especially when they were broke, hungry and under a lot of stress. Some ghetto people liked it when someone was a bad man, a gangster, or a thug, so they could protect them from other bad guys from other parts or neighbourhoods. That's also what I meant when I said that they could be quite hypocritical as well. They liked it when bad men displayed area leadership, so when someone was feuding with someone else, they could come up with a solution for the problem. So, the fact of the matter was some ghetto people did like thieves and robbers if they could bring the thieving goods to share with them.

CHAPTER 3

School Days

My siblings and I went to Windward Road All Age School, just off the main road. The school grade level started at Grade 1 and went all the way up to Grade 8. That school was well renowned to have some of the smartest and brightest prospects in attendance, whether they were teachers or students. Windward Road had some of the best artists, athletes and dancers on the whole island. One thing that I know for sure is true is that the good Lord never forsakes the poor, and he finds a way to give them strength and perseverance to carry on.

The Lord always seems to have a blessing for the most poverty-stricken kind of people just trying to survive. It's a proven fact that some of the best athletes and some of the most extraordinarily successful people in the world came from nothing and had nothing to show but their hard work, dedication, and faith in God. It was their faith that kept them going and their determination to make something of themselves. Some people recognize the struggle at an early age in life and embrace the challenges ahead, while some that were less fortunate gave up too soon on life and have fallen by the wayside.

My former school had people in attendance that came from far and near. Students came from the east, west, north and south. They came from many distances and many walks of life in Jamaica just to attend Windward Road All Age School. They made the effort to attend that school so that they could get a good education and be taught discipline and self-worth. Windward Road All Age School was a very special school for me. That place really began to shape and mould me in a positive light. Some of the teachers of that establishment really tried to care as long as students were willing to learn and take proper steps necessary to grow to be a better person. It wasn't easy, but I have learned lessons along the way.

Some of those teachers regularly expressed concern for their students' well-being, education, and self-esteem. Every morning before devotion some of the teachers would inspect the students' hands, uniforms, and shoes. They would look at your hands and nails to see if they were dirty or not and also look if students were wearing nail polish because it was forbidden.

They made it their point of duty to make observations about our uniforms and judge whose were worn out and had holes in them and whose need to be replaced as soon as possible. We had to make sure that there wasn't a hem out of place, for situations like that may have led to embarrassment or worse. There were harsh and stiff punishments from time to time. That was the kind of establishment that school was running; most schools in Jamaica were usually run according to certain rules like that.

My siblings and I made sure that our hands and nails were always clean. Some teachers at times would commend us for keenly following the rules. When they complimented us, we just took it and ran with it quickly. You know what they say, out of sight is out of mind. I would sometimes feel sorry for some of my fellow students and friends though, for the teachers would become very vocal with their opinions and the way that they felt and that was embarrassing for others.

The teachers would judge some of the students unfairly and a bit harshly to determine whether they were from good homes or from some rough neighbourhoods and upbringings. They could be a bit judgemental, but that was just the way it was. They would judge who was from a slightly less desirable upbringing and where they came from; some places were a bit more ravaged than others. So, students were sometimes misrepresented or misconstrued and were sometimes judged harshly by some teachers by the way they looked or the way they acted in public settings or because of where they lived and came from.

It was stereotypical of the teachers to judge others in that sort of manner, to determine who was being taken care of or who was being neglected. While the teachers were going through their daily interrogations, they would occasionally skip me and my sisters because we were judged to be clean in their eyes at times. I was happy that most of the time we didn't have to experience that kind of negative rhetoric and verbal assaults in the mornings at devotion.

They would also tell us that we were good most of the time, even though we had had a few runs in with them before. Whether they were criticizing us or making references to a clip that we used in our hair, a hem that was pulling out of a garment, or a pleat that wasn't pressed neatly, we had a few little runs in with them.

I got in trouble once for my uniform dress hem because it was not up to par one morning while I was lined up outside of the school yard for devotion. I had noticed the hem on my dress was pulling out at school from the day before, but I neglected to tell my mother that night. Since my mother was working the evening shift at the hospital and she had gotten home late the night before, I was sleeping by the time she got home. So, when I woke up the next day for school, I tried fixing the hem by myself with a few bobby pins. I thought no one would notice it. Well, my expectations were short-lived, because a teacher by the name of Mrs. Barrett approached me and started calling me out for my uniform. She told me how terrible and disorderly I looked. I mean she went ham on me and will never forget it. I was totally embarrassed, and I felt disgraceful. Everyone began to look at me and the whole episode brought some attention that I did not want. I suppose Mrs. Barrett was right in the sense that my uniform that day was a hot mess. I had forgotten to tell my mother the night before that my uniform hems were pulled out. Well, I never made that mistake again, for I didn't want to feel that type of humiliation again. I never wanted my feet to be held in that kind of fire ever again.

Most of the time students felt stigma; their body language and facial expression said it all. I felt bad for them because the teachers' words were most unkind and harsh at times. The teachers' methods of communication were justifiable to them because they felt that it was an effective approach to things in all aspects. They felt that it worked for most of the students because some of them never made that mistake again of coming to school unprepared for learning or inspection. Some students made sure that they looked clean and neat all the time and represented themselves and the school well.

Mr. and Mrs. Duncan were the principal and vice-principal of Windward Road All Age School in those days, for as far back as I can remember. They were husband and wife, the rarest of its kind and form, for husband and wife to share authority and dictatorship in one school. Make no mistake about it, they were the ones not to be messed with for one second or get on their bad side. Every student that attended that school got the memo that they were highly feared, make no mistake about that.

Most people that I knew always tried to follow the rules and guidelines of going to class, doing the work, not skipping class, and always keeping the peace. Most of all students were not to bring any form of weapons to school, like knives or guns. In a way, the school was very diverse and dynamic because students from all over had to try their best to get along with each other regardless of their differences with each other's neighbourhoods. After all, if you violated those rules there would be some serious repercussions from Mr. and Mrs. Duncan. In other words, the Duncan's would beat the living daylights out of the students until the students understood not to mess up.

My impression of Mr. and Mrs. Duncan were that they were each as tough as tooth and nail. They operated like two bad cops. They were both strict and enjoying giving harsh punishments. They were also up for the challenge of giving a good ass whooping each time; they were unapologetic about that too. Their methods of punishment were to beat students with rubber belts made of spare rubber tires, not to mention the electrical wiring used to string up light poles that was often used to beat students as well. It was insane if you think about it.

I had often heard stories about the Duncan's, but the first time that I witnessed the wrath of the Duncan's was on one Wednesday morning when my teacher Mrs. Barns asked me to take the attendance down to the office. After handing the attendance to the secretary, I was just leaving the office to head back to class when to my surprise I saw Mrs. Duncan arguing with a male student by the name of Donavon. Mrs. Duncan at the time looked angry and upset at him, her demeanour was rather mad, and she looked like a ferocious lion that would devour your flesh instantly. That morning she looked vicious and was ready to pounce. I don't know what he did that day, and I was in no position to find out either. My intuition was telling me that morning to get the hell out of there quickly. I got out of that office with a sense of urgency because I didn't want to be any part of that, and I didn't want to be caught up in any of the crossfire.

As I was heading out of the office, the next thing I knew Mrs. Duncan was telling Donavan to step out of the office with her. As soon as I heard those words telling him that, I thought to myself that this must be serious, and that Donavon was surely going to get some good ass whooping. So, he complied slowly and made his way out of the office. The next thing I knew, she began to beat him with a tall, thick black piece of slinky rubber-tire-belt-like object. Mrs. Duncan began to strike Donavon hard with force repeatedly with that rubber belt and she was beating him constantly all over his hands, back and shoulders. She showed him no mercy, beating the living daylights out of him as her way of handing out his punishment.

He began to cry out loud, hollering, weeping, and wailing, as she began to strike him with aggressive slaps across his body. The sight of what had transpired in front of me scared me that day. I would never want to be on her bad side because Mrs. Duncan seemed very cruel. In a sense, she had driven fear inside me. Poor Donavon, I began to feel sorry for him almost like I wanted to help but I couldn't even help myself. I was in shock and mortified with the level of aggression and force she had displayed. That young man's beating was rough and to think that Mrs. Duncan and her husband had often beaten students in that way was frankly disturbing. I'm pretty sure that most students were physically scarred for life by them both.

That day I finally figured out and understood the reasons why the whole school disliked them and spoke poorly about the Duncan's all the time. No one had anything good or positive to say about them in any way. They were greatly disliked by others; there was no secret about it. The two of them were like two peas in a pod. They reminded me of two mongooses on the prowl for snakes, and the students were the snakes. But technically the principals were the snakes.

There was one day that Mrs. Duncan had beaten a student so hard that her wig fell off. When that happened, the students, including my sister Royal, that had witnessed the ordeal said it was quite a sight to behold. My sister Royal said that she and her friends laughed so hard because Mrs. Duncan had no hair on her head, not even a strand. My sister and her friends said that it was the funniest thing ever and that the look on Mrs. Duncan's face was priceless. They said when her wig fell off it was pure humiliation and embarrassment for Mrs. Duncan, but it was also magical at the same time for the students for that day Royal and friends found out one of Mrs. Duncan's secrets: the vice-principal had absolutely no hair on her head. Perhaps she was sick, they had thought, and not long after that, the rumours about her mishap began to circulate. From there on after, whenever a student saw Mrs. Duncan that is all that they would make mention of.

Most of the time the Duncan's' disciplinary methods did not resonate well with the parents of the students whom they had scolded. There were times when mothers and fathers came down to Windward Road All Age School to argue with the Duncan's over their use of physical restraints with their sons and daughters. Sometimes the conversations would get so heated in front of the school you were pretty sure that someone was going to throw the first blow and that it was going to get violent in a hurry. Parents would come from all over to defend their children's rights, especially when their sons and daughters had bruises, scars and marks all over their bodies.

The Duncan's were masterful at their craft, and they were truly wicked, quite cruel, and a ruthless pair. They were simply made for each other, not because they were husband and wife, but because they portrayed similar characteristics and traits to each other. They made it their point of duty to drive fear into the minds of the students. It was rumoured that Mr. Duncan had once been a policeman. I don't know if there was any truth in that, but that was the rumour for years. They even resembled each other; he was bald, and she was bald underneath her wig.

Many parents were angry and demanded full explanations from the Duncan's as to what the bloody hell had happened to their children. The parents were practically butting heads with the Duncan's, but of course, nothing came out of it. Parents had to tolerate the situation; you either put up or shipped out. That was the Duncan's' nasty attitude and dirty mentality towards others, as if they were superior. But nothing ever came of those battles because the Duncan's usually got away with everything. Even the teachers punished the students by humiliating them in front of the classroom. They would make students stand on one foot while holding the other foot and pulling their ears with one arm for a long time. They would also make students get down on their knees to rest on soda bottle covers, almost like beer bottle covers. The look on their faces indicated they were in excruciating pain. When the punishment was over, the soda bottle cover made indents on their knees. It was just the typical ancient rules of the government of Jamaica and both the teachers and principals abused their privileged power for many years . . . the power that was given to them.

I suppose school should be a place where you're able to learn new things and express new ideas about people, places, things, and time. School is a place where should bond with peers, groups, and sometimes teachers on a social and intellectual level about things and everyday life. It should be a haven for all students, where you are free to mingle and have some innocent fun, with no apology or even worry about physical punishment from anyone. Of course, along with life's everyday struggles and unexpected retribution and tribulations, I tell you, the struggles are real.

CHAPTER 4

Friendships Formed While Others Are Short-Lived

I have met a lot of smart and interesting people along the way, particularly friends when I was growing up and throughout my school years in Jamaica. My school friends and acquaintances were Tamara, Tonya, Marsha, and Sharita. There was also Trisha, but we never really were friends like that. We just happened to run and be in the same social circle. Marsha and Sherita were first cousins. I surrounded myself with happy, fun, and jovial people at times. Some of those girls I considered my social friends, and that was just to mention a few. We were young impressionable girls who were stress-free and not worried at times about life problems and expectations.

I got along with the girls because we respected each other—at least some of them for the most part. I suppose that we all had some things in common, like we were all raised in different hoods, so we understood the struggles that each one of our parents and to go through to take care of us daily. What I most enjoyed about those friendships was that we hardly had any serious quarrels or issues. The girls weren't too catty. I mean maybe sometimes we would have our occasional silly disputes about silly things, but it was never anything serious. They were well-behaved girls most of the time.

Tamara and Tonya, I considered my best friends for life. Yep, those were my girls. I knew Tamara from preschool and Tonya from Grade 1. I shared more of a special bond with those two than the rest. I considered them my closest and most loyal subjects and friends, for they were near and dear to me. They were almost like my own sisters in a way because we shared many secrets like bosom buddies. Tamara and I would walk to and from school together each day. During the lunch hours we would eat our lunches together about half of the time. I would say that she went home fifty percent of the time. The other fifty percent of the time I was buying. That way she could stay at school for lunch and hang out with the rest of the gang.

My money and sharing what I had, and certain things of that nature, were always good enough for my friends. I never thought twice about caring and sharing what I had with my friends. I would like to think that they would have done the same thing for me. For they say good friends are better than pocket money. Good friends cannot be bought or sold; some are simply priceless, or at least that is what I thought.

Most of my little friends always tried their best to have their little lunch money before the weekend was finished to rotate back in the upcoming week for school. Most parents made sure that their children were prepared for the upcoming week to fly high or low. My friend Tamara was not the type of girl that would walk with lunch or have lunch money to purchase lunch daily. She would carry lunch money to school now and then, especially on the days when she visited her father's home. Sometimes Tamara would go home for lunch, but on the days when she didn't go home for lunch, I would take the liberty to treat her to lunch. Naturally, lunchtime was always the best time of the day, especially when there was some sweet sugar bun and cherry milk on the menu.

Those were the good old days, when sweet sugar buns and cherry milk were served up at school in every classroom for free, courtesy of the Government of Jamaica. That was when things were nice, and the government was caring and giving back to the people of Jamaica. Unfortunately, that compassion and giving back don't exist anymore. Besides, some of the teachers acted selfishly by not giving away the free food or making sure that the children received it. When the crates of sweet buns and cherry milk were brought to the classroom the teachers would give away a small amount and kept the rest for themselves. Some teachers were just too greedy with the free food, and there was enough for everyone more times over.

On other lunch days when I convinced Tamara to stay at school for lunch, I would buy her some corn bread and butter, which she enjoyed very much. On other days she would go home for lunch because it was cost-efficient for her and her family at times. Sometimes I even went home with her for lunch when she invited me. Her mother was always kind to me and was always a gracious host. We would sometimes eat corn meal or oats porridge with some crackers. Some days we would eat plantains with bread and a refreshing tall glass of fruit juice and sometimes ice-cold lemonade. Then we would head back to school with urgency because we couldn't afford to be late getting back to our studies.

One thing I couldn't figure out and will never understand with this friendship was when Tamara and I were in the fifth grade, and we had to do a major exam before we entered the sixth grade. The exam was called the Common Entrance or the CE. It was usually taken by boys and girls aged eleven or thirteen in Jamaica. The test would consist of math, English, and science. The test became a pivotal point of our young lives to determine our future because the results would inform which high school we could enter. The higher the score, the better our chances were to go to a senior independent school.

So, it was in the student's best interest and ability to do well and for the teachers to make sure that they had prepared their pupils as well. The senior schools in the region you lived in were responsible for marking the test. Students' results were usually printed in the

Local Gleaner with information about what school they were selected to go to. Most people in Jamaica usually bought the Local Gleaner that day. If they didn't buy it any other day, well, on that day they usually did.

People naturally wanted to know who had and had not passed their CE. Students that time of year were always feeling immense pressure to do well academically. If you passed, then great for you; it meant that your future looked bright. But if you didn't pass, then you were considered and labelled as a dunce by others. Well, the moment of truth had arrived. When the newspaper printed that day, my name was nowhere to be found. I searched high and low, but my name was still nowhere to be found.

I knew from that moment on that I didn't pass the exam and the sooner I had accepted the facts the better it would be for me. I began feeling like a failure and that I had somehow let down my mother and the rest of my family. I felt anger, sadness, and embarrassment and was truly ashamed. I was feeling all sorts of stigmas mixed up in one. However, some of my closest friends didn't pass either. Some of my good friends passed the exam, while some flunked it just like me. My best friend Tamara passed. I was very happy for her but still sad for myself. I knew that I had let that opportunity slip by, but at least I had a chance to do it again at thirteen years of age.

That day while I was sitting on my verandah reflecting on what I could have done better on the exam, I saw a friendly face strolling by outside my gate. It was none other than my best friend Tamara. Just the person that I needed to see to cheer me up, I had thought. Besides, I was glad to see her because I wanted to congratulate her on passing the exam. But it was not to be. I was calling her to get her attention to slow down, but she just ignored me and kept on walking. The reason why I knew that she was ignoring me was that we had made eye contact with each other. She looked straight at me and kept on walking. I called her name several times and she pretended as if she didn't hear me. Perhaps she had instantaneously grown out of our friendship since passing the CE. It seemed as if home girl had cancelled me, and my feelings were hurt like hell.

My other friend Tonya did not live anywhere remotely close to where I lived. She lived farther east, going back to town to the Coronation Market in downtown Kingston. Tonya had now become one of my closest friends, as well my closest confidant, since I was cancelled by Tamara. I had grown to understand Tonya and she understood me as well. I trusted her with everything. I considered her my bosom buddy. She would reason with me and tell me everything, and I think that everyone needs one of those types of friends in their lives and corners now and then for sure.

The truth of the matter is that I admired each one of my friends and the different qualities that they each possessed. Sharita was quite articulate, and she knew how to draw and paint well. She had great visualization of the subject like no other, whether it was a person or an object, and she just knew how to capture it on paper or canvas. I on the other hand could not draw even if my life depended on it. I wasn't any good at that sort of stuff. It just wasn't my thing. Dancing and my level of flexibility on the hand was my thing. I was good at it as everyone else knew. I was proud of that; I was fortunate that God hadn't left me hanging out to dry and had blessed me with that kind of natural and raw talent.

Marsha and Sherita were cool girls, but Marsha had a lot of flaws. Her biggest flaw was that she was a terrible liar. She lied about just about everything, and she also enjoyed telling tales. In other words, she had a lying tongue, and she had many issues telling the truth about the simplest things, whether school-related or family-related. She made it impossible for me to believe her at times, even though I so wanted to believe her. Apart from her lies she was a lovely girl. Nobody's perfect. You just don't unfriend someone because they are faulty. She tried too hard to be accepted by others when all she had to do was be herself. It was that side of her that everyone loved and respected. I just wished she could have too.

I must admit she sure was a funny girl. Other times some of her stories and reasoning I couldn't make much sense of because she made it so impossible for the rest of us to believe her at times. She would always have a straight face when making up stories, sort of like a blank stare or a poker face. I know in my heart and soul that she told us at times some untrue stories. But I still loved her unconditionally and respected her in so many ways. Mainly and most importantly she was my friend. After all, we all have our flaws—I do too—because no one is perfect but the good Lord himself.

There was a girl named Trisha and she became my classmate over the years, ever since we were in the first grade. When I was in Grade 1, she was too, and we were in the same classroom from then all the way up to Grade 6. I just never seemed to get a break from being in the same class with her. I would like to have considered her my good friend, but for some weird reason, it wasn't to be so. That ship had sailed many grades before with that friendship. It was beyond my control. The older I got I realized it was a pity that we were not closer than expected because I had known her since Grade 1.

I just couldn't get a break with Trisha at all. The girl was not warm or welcoming. Whenever I was around, she appeared to be annoyed, and she would have a frown on her face and all sorts of other facial expressions. She acted as if she smelled shit or something. I knew this because of her bad attitude, poor body language and demeanour. Every time she saw me her feathers appeared to be ruffled somehow. The truth of the matter was she didn't impress me much, and I was very annoyed with her behaviour as well. I certainly didn't put up with that kind of nonsense, whether it's with Trisha or anyone else. That's the difference between me and some of my friends; I had no problem expressing myself. I had no problem being assertive. Sometimes I would also keep my cool and keep it together and all.

That girl was a piece of work, and she took great pleasure in criticizing people. She made it her duty to put others down, especially when she didn't get her way, sort of like a bully. She was like a Negative Nelly and a Debbie Downer all in one, all mixed up in one pile of shaving cream. Those were some of the reasons why we were butting heads with each other. We didn't get along at all. It was always like a competition or a duel between us over the years. For sure that friendship was a challenge and a power struggle for me I must say!

I get it the girl disliked me and I was okay with that. Perhaps in a way, we both had strong personalities, but we most certainly were two different people. We had absolutely nothing in common except that we were both friends with Tonya, and a lot of time Tonya was put in the uncomfortable position of having to choose sides. One thing I know for sure is that not everyone will like everyone, especially with a circle of friends. I was never Trisha's favourite cup of tea, and she was never mine. It was as simple as that. Of course, I considered her more of a friend to Tonya than to me, which was fine. As a matter of fact, I had no problems sharing my friends with others, but she had a problem with the friendship that Tonya and I shared.

CHAPTER 5

Death and Some Near-Death Experiences

I would often see or hear stories of people getting shot with a gun or chopped with a machete, and most of the time those incidents would lead to fatalities. Living in the garrison's brutality at times came with the territory. I would also hear stories of people getting worked over by Voodoo or witchcraft by people in possession of supernatural powers. I have seen with my own eyes successful people that were supposed to be the talk of the town go mad for no apparent reason. For example, there was a young man that lived across the street from us by the name of Wayne. He once attended the University of the West Indies. He was studying become to a medical doctor. He was a handsome young man who was well educated and filled with a lot of potential to succeed. It was evident that he had a lot going for him. Now everyone knows that to even be accepted to the University of the West Indies you must be highly intelligent.

Wayne became a mad man. Whenever I used to pass by him when I was going to school or coming home from other places, I would see him, and he would give me that uncomfortable stare, just laughing and talking to himself. I would occasionally say hello to him, but he never once replied to me or anyone else that I knew. There were days when I had to pass him by and I felt uneasy as if he were going to rush and attack me, but he never did. When it comes to a mad man you just never quite know what you are dealing with. His behaviour was just so bizarre at times that we were told by friends and family to stay away from him. Many people had concluded that it was Voodoo and that someone had put a spell on him or something. Perhaps it was just a severe case of schizophrenia. Rumour had it that Wayne was examined by many different doctors, but none gave a clear-cut explanation as to what was wrong with him. They could not tell what was wrong with him. There are just some things in life that are hard to understand. We just can't comprehend them at times and never will. If the light exists, so does the darkness.

I once knew a friend of both my parents, it was a man by the name of Jack, and his tragic death will never be forgotten. Jack was a very hard-working man that did anything and everything for his two children. Par was his daughter and Noelle was his son. He was a good and decent man and I respected him because he was honest and kind to everyone. Jack had a wife once, but apparently, she died when Noelle was a baby. She had died from an unknown illness, and he never had the urge to remarry anyone else. My sister Andrea and I would hang with Noelle from time to time at his house in his backyard. We didn't hang with his older sister Par so much because she was much older. She was more in the age group of my brother Audley and my sister Angelica. I loved hanging out with Noelle and keeping his company because he was a good friend to me and my sister. He made us laugh a lot and he just loved to gossip and chat about other people. Call me hypocritical, but I enjoyed every minute of it. He was one of those friends that could turn rain into sunshine. He was just a delight to have around.

What I also liked about Noelle was that he was very charismatic and didn't take himself too seriously. He was a bit flamboyant and very much on the eccentric side, but I didn't mind. I didn't care or judge him nor his personality, because he was a wonderful and thoughtful person and I enjoyed being around him. My sisters did too. Tea for some, coffee or lemonade for others.

I must say though the only downfall his father Jack had was that he was a heavy drinker, and he loved that Jamaican white rum. After work, you could always find him at the local bar down the road on the main street. The main street local bar was his favourite place to be more than his home. He was an alcoholic and a noisy drunk at times; we would hear him in our home as he was making his way up the street to go home. But a lot of people still cared for him and respected him, because he was a good person regardless of his way of life.

Some said that Jack never really got over the death of his wife and the burden that he bore raising those kids by himself. I suppose everyone has their different ways of dealing with tragedy. Some people ease their pain by drinking while others might smoke. No one ever really knows how a person feels or experiences until they walk a mile in that person's shoe. Perhaps he just drank all the time to mend a broken heart and that led him to alcoholism.

One early morning around five thirty, I woke up to a commotion. I heard my mother waking up my older brother and sister telling them that a man was shouting in the streets, "They killed Jack! They killed Jack!" The man that was shouting practically woke up the whole neighbourhood. He was shouting hysterically in the streets that Jack was dead and that seemed to get everyone's attention. So, I realized that something bad had transpired. I immediately fell out of my bed, and I woke up the rest of my siblings so we could have a better understanding of what was going on.

We all went outside on the verandah together that morning. My mother never minded that we were all woken up because the whole neighbourhood had been for that matter. Then we saw the man continuously yelling such distressing news. We were hoping that it was not true. But we had no way of proving it until others had made their way down the street to confirm Jack's lifeless body lying on the ground. It was still dark during that time early morning and I and my family couldn't wait until daybreak to go and look at the body for ourselves. I began to wonder if what the man was saying was a pure fabrication or if there were any truth to it all. Maybe the man had consumed too much alcohol, I thought. We all began to speculate. Then I began to think about Noelle and if they had heard any news of what was going on.

As I sat there, I began to feel a bit nostalgic, scared and sad. I also was feeling tired and worrisome too, and all kinds of emotions began running through my head. I was just hoping and praying that Jack was all right. We must have sat on the verandah for the next two hours. By that time the shouting man had gone away. We were up until daybreak and the sun came out. By then the bad news has been confirmed by others. The tragic and sad news about Jack had spread and people came out of their houses to talk about what had happened, and the neighbour that lived across the street from us, Mr. Mass, had confirmed that the news about Jack was, in fact, true. Jack had died.

Witnesses said that Jack and two men got into an argument over money at the bar. The men wanted money from Jack, but Jack refused to give them any of his hard-earned money. So, the two men argued with Jack and began to pat him down. This led to a major scuffle. After the incident, the two men decided immediately to leave the bar and witnesses thought that was the end of that altercation.

It was almost closing time and the bartender had announced it was last round. Then around twelve thirty or so, when Jack took his last shot of white rum, he decided to go home. It wasn't out of Jack's character to leave when it was closing time; it was in his nature to do so. Anyway, Jack proceeded to exit the bar to make his way home.

Then as Jack began to make his way home up the street, the two men that had the scuffle with Jack earlier on started to follow him home. Jack was unprepared for round two with the men because witnesses say that he was as drunk as a skunk. The two men began to argue with Jack once again and the two men got physical with him.

They started hitting Jack and punching him in his head, face and all over. They beat him and hit him so hard that he lost his balance and pitched over to the ground. Then the two men proceeded to kick him and stomp him on top of his head. Witnesses said that Jack didn't even put up a fight because he was too intoxicated to do so.

They shamelessly beat Jack to a bloody pulp. Jack was lying on the ground breathless, and no one had the guts to go to his rescue. The two men began searching Jack's pockets and took all of his belongings, including his money. The two thieves even went as far as stealing the gold tooth from the front of his mouth. He was not only dead, but he lay there toothless as well. How despicable, wicked, and shameful of those two thieves in every aspect.

That is the ultimate in utter disrespect, whether for the living or the dead. No one should be subjected to or endure that type of pain, while living, dying or dead. Can you imagine someone viciously invading your personal space and to add further insult pulling one tooth of gold out of your mouth for their personal gain? There are a few choice words that can describe those two men that killed Jack. They were truly barbaric.

So that morning I was getting ready for school. My brothers and sisters were highly encouraged by my mother to try and carry on the rest of the day and not to worry our little heads and think too much. Just a little bit before we left for school I and my sisters Andrea and Royal and brother Ian made a pact that we would head down the street to the scene of the crime to have a look for ourselves.

So, we headed down the street. When we got there, Jack's body, including his face, was covered with a sheet. Thank goodness that someone was gracious enough and had the decency to cover him up. At that moment in time, I remained optimistic that there were some good people still left in this world. I had never experienced death like that before, especially of someone that was a close family friend. I remember a lot of people standing around gossiping and speculating as to why a good man like Jack had to die so soon and in such a horrible way. Some were even speculating with all kinds of notions that it was a robbery gone wrong.

People started gathering one by one to look at Jack's dead body; some of them started lifting the sheet off to take a glance at his face. My sister Royal and I went first to take a glance, then Andrea and Angelica did. My brothers followed suit shortly thereafter, except my younger brother Ian; he was too scared to look. That was perfectly understandable. He would have probably had nightmares anyway. My older brother Audley looked, and he never flinched a muscle. Perhaps his stomach was stronger than the rest of ours.

I couldn't stop thinking about Noelle and what he must have been feeling; his world had been turned upside down. First to lose a mother at such a young age and then a father, I wish I could have consoled him then and told him how truly sorry I was for his loss and that life would truly somehow get better in due time.

The truth of the matter is the whole experience shook me up. It began to ride on my feelings and emotions. I felt anxious, sad, angry, and scared that people were here today and gone tomorrow. I realized life could be taken away from you at any given time; you just wouldn't know when your turn was coming, especially in a hostile environment.

In my heart I felt bad for Noelle and his sister, seeing Jack's lifeless body just lying there on the ground. It's an image that will forever be planted in my head. Later that day my family and I expressed our deepest condolences to Noelle and his sister, Par. We also told them that if there was anything that we could do to help to ease their burden and stress to please feel free to let us know. They were pretty shaken up and they seemed incoherent at the time. I can't say that I blame them. Who feels it knows it?

But to be very frank, my friendship with Noelle was never the same as time passed. I could see the hurt in his face and his body language said it all. Whenever we made eye contact with each other or even had a conversation it would remain short and brief, and he would always look away. After a while, Noelle began to ostracize himself from my family and me and the rest of his friends that cared about him in our neighbourhood. It was clear that he was going through depression and some type of stigma in that regard, which was understandable. After months and time had passed by Noelle wasn't coming to school much; eventually, he dropped out at a young age to fend for himself and Par, but there was nothing that I could've done. I was too young and certainly quite helpless.

I went through my close encounters with death at a young age. I once had a lovely neighbour by the name of Aunt Flores. She lived next door to me in the house next to the back of our yard. Aunt Flores was quite lovely and kind to me and my family. She was almost like the grandmother I never had. She was always warm and welcoming to my siblings and me. We would always jump the fence that was connected to both of our houses at the back of the yard to get over to her place. She would welcome us with open arms any time of the day, weekends included. Her home was almost like my second home. I would prance around inside and out as if it were my own house.

I would go to her house to watch television often, day and night, which was of course nice for me because she was practically like family anyhow. I can't ever recall a single time that Aunt Flores had ever shown me a bad face or given me the slightest inclination that I wasn't wanted around. May the good Lord bless her heart because she was a good person.

Aunt Flores at the time had a nice big screen-coloured television that I preferred watching, strictly for entertainment purposes to my liking. That coloured television lewas more modern, just the way I liked it. The family television that I had at home was more of the old fashion, black-and-white television with just a touch of gray. Even though I did not have a coloured television at home, my family and I enjoyed the old classic silver screen movies. Coloured television was introduced to me, and I was hooked every step of the way. I also began seeing things from a different perspective and seeing things that were out there in this world.

Aunt Flores became the grandmother that I never had. That wonderful lady treated me like I was one of her own and she was like that with every one of my siblings too. For whatever it is worth I will forever be grateful for that. My mother treated her well too; that's what good neighbours do. I can clearly remember whenever my mother went to the market on Saturday mornings, she would sometimes pick up a few extra fruits, vegetables, and meat items and when she came home, she would share her grocery basket with Aunt Flores. They were always appreciative of each other, so it was a great friendship from both sides of the fence.

I suppose being at Aunt Flores's house, even on days when my mother had to work late, gave me peace of mind. Her specialty most of the time was giving me powdered milk in a cup with sugar, but hey I can't complain, I didn't mind it at all. It could have been much worse. Milk powder was the least of my worries. Being in her home gave me a chance to reflect on my young life with some clarity.

I also enjoyed shooting marbles with Aunt Flores's great-grandson, Omar, whenever he came over, right underneath the soursop tree in the yard. Omar was very competitive when it came to racing and shooting marbles. But then again so was I. He sure knew how to pluck the living daylights out of those marbles; he was very good at it. It was merely impossible to beat him at marbles. There is one thing that I know for sure that he couldn't beat me at though: running against me in a race. I would beat him in sprinting time after time in his granny's backyard. I guess it was just the competitive spirit within me. Today for you, tomorrow for me.

One sunny Saturday afternoon around quarter past twelve, I decided that I would give Aunt Flores a friendly visit. So, I jumped the fence and spent an hour and a half that day at her house. I decided to leave early because Aunt Flores was feeling tired at the time, and she wanted to take a nap. I was also getting a bit bored as well. There was no one else left to keep me company there anyway. So, I decided that it was time to go home and not overstay my welcome. That afternoon I was feeling a bit reluctant about which way I was going to take to get home. I just didn't have the strength to jump back over the fence. So, I made a conscious decision to take the long way home. It usually took me three minutes or so to get home that way. I gathered myself and told Aunt Flores goodbye and headed out of her front gate.

As I exited and closed the front gate I started walking home and just a few feet from Aunt Flores's yard I saw numerous people running and looking like they were taking cover. I remember seeing Miss Alga ducking and taking cover. She was a long-time family friend of my father's but not so much my mother's. Miss Alga took cover and was hitched up and squeezing herself tightly in the corner of the street wall. She was desperately cringing up and trying to make herself look small, almost as if she were waiting and hoping for a miracle to be invisible.

Around the same time, I saw a gunman running with heavy machinery in his hand. He appeared to be limping and blood was dripping from his leg. It was evident that he was hurt. It looked as if he had a serious injury going on with his foot. This all transpired just a few moments after I came out of the yard. It never dawned on me at that moment to just turn back to go to Aunty Flores's house and just jump the fence to go home. Everyone that I saw on the street that day was just running and screaming hysterically. Some of them seemed desperate to find cover just like Miss Alga, whether it was getting down flat on the concrete sidewalks or hiding in someone else's backyard just to make the gunman pass by peacefully. One could only hope in that situation that the gunman was not trigger happy and that he didn't get carried away by harming innocent bystanders—not that it would make any difference to some criminals.

Everything was happening so fast around me, and I didn't have time or even know how to make a conscious decision about what to do with myself. Miss Alga didn't give me any heads up or even try to warn me that I was in the middle of a shootout or how to protect myself. I soon learned that it was every person for themselves during that ordeal. The silly, foolish, and helpless girl that was inside of me kept on walking and walking instead of getting down flat on the ground to avoid any bullets that may come my way. I only had one thing on my mind that day—to get home to my family. It seemed to be the longest three minutes that I had ever taken to get home with all that was going on. Everything was happening so fast, and I kept on walking until I reached my destination. As soon as I reached the front of my yard gate on the street, I heard shots firing. When I looked up, I saw another gunman running out of Mr. Mass's meat shop firing gunshots and then his neighbour Mr. Cloaf started firing back at him when he was running up the street.

As the shots were firing nonstop, I remember my mother and sisters Andrea and Royal shouting constantly and saying, "Bluff, get down! Get down and hide underneath the car!" At that exact moment, I realized that my life was in danger. It was as if the light bulb had finally turned on inside my head. So, I followed my family's instructions and immediately ducked and hid beside the car because I just couldn't bring myself to get under Mr. Chappy's car. Mr. Chappy was Baps's boyfriend and Baps resided inside my family's home.

I must have lain beside that car for a whole five minutes until the dust had settled or when I thought it was safe for me to come out of hiding. I remember hearing the voice of my mother telling me to run. So, I ran as fast as I could inside of my yard, straight onto the verandah, right into my room, and locked the door. I sat in my room crying, sobbing, and praying. I was wondering and pondering to myself what if I had gotten shot or possibly died. I thanked the good Lord, my heavenly father, for protecting me and saving me from harm's way that day. It took a while for me to finally come out of my room for supper that evening. My mother along with the rest of my family told me that when the police came to investigate the scene of the crime, they did some forensic testing and found some shell casings from shots fired earlier. The casings were underneath Chappy's car. Hearing that news certainly didn't make me feel any better. It only made matters worse for me and my thought process. So, my mother and my siblings consoled me for the rest of the evening and gave me words of encouragement to stay positive.

I was traumatized for a few weeks. I wouldn't leave my house to go anywhere unless it was to school. The truth is I was feeling scared, and I didn't feel carefree like before. Even when it came to going to school, I had to have courage and put on a brave front. I had no choice but to get tough, persevere, and push on. I had to look myself in the mirror and tell myself it was going to be all right. I even stopped going to Aunt Flores's home for one whole month. I started staying home more often. It was the right thing for me to do personally because anything can happen to anyone at any given time, and I was always expecting the unexpected to happen from there on.

CHAPTER 6

Bloodshed and Political Warfare

It was 1983 and that was also the election year. During that time things could become very ominous and violent. As a child it was very difficult to travel from place to place or even attend school, because of all the political aspects that surrounded my communities. People in my surroundings and all over Jamaica were dying of gun violence and dropping like flies. The elections were always brutal and very wicked because innocent people were always dying. I couldn't attend school because people in the community were constantly having violent stand-offs between police or rival gangs. It was the People's National Party (PNP) versus the Jamaica Labour Party (JLP).

The streets in my neighbourhood were blocked with trees, wood, zinc, metal, mattresses, old pans, and pretty much the whole kitchen sink. Tires were constantly burning, and the people blocked the middle of the roads in the communities with pretty much whatever they found and put out there in the streets. It also acted as a roadblock because no one was allowed to leave the community or come into the community because of political confrontation and death associated with rivals and the thirst for power by the opposition in the election year.

The people in my neighbourhood were PNP supporters and they had a legitimate reason for some of the roadblocks in the streets to protect the people from outsiders like the JLP. Sometimes the police would patrol and intervene to protect others from harming the community in which we lived. A lot of unstable environments had quickly developed all over Jamaica. An epidemic of violence at that time was fostered in Jamaica and the people, including me and my family, grew scared because of the violence and the number of people that were dying daily in my community and other neighbourhoods all over Kingston, Jamaica.

The PNPs didn't like the JLPs and vice versa. There were no hidden secrets about that, and innocent people were caught some of the time in the crossfire of both parties because people and their ignorance towards others led to continuous clashes. As a youth, I couldn't wait to see the day when it was all over. It made me feel unsafe and afraid, whether it was day or especially night. The elections brought about a lot of economic struggles and failures in Jamaica and a lot of people suffered in vain because of political motives and agendas affiliated with and surrounded by both parties. The rhetoric and message presented by the JLPs were very combative to the Jamaican people, and we lived in fear because of its politics and governing system. Everyone that I knew had their radios and televisions sets on because everyone wanted to be in the know as to what was happening to the country. About one hundred people were murdered leading up to the election and those were truly some perils for me all in the name of politics and politicking!

Later that year, the Jamaica Labour Party won the election, and the loss was a massive blow to the People's National Party and all people in my community. I was relieved that it was finally over and that the people of Jamaica could pick up the pieces, stay strong, and carry on as difficult as that was. I was relieved because my mother could get back to work, and we could finally go back to school after so many weeks of not being able to go. I thanked God that it was over and there was finally some light at the end of that saga. I hoped to God that I would never have to experience that kind of ordeal ever again.

Say Something, Say Goodbye

A few years had gone by since my father had gone to Canada, and the relationship between he and my mother had become strained. He was not corresponding with her at all, whether by writing letters or by making a mere telephone call. After a while, my mother was the one that had to be the ultimate breadwinner for our family's survival, and she did very well with a lot of social graces. She was determined not to let people laugh at us and look down on us. She was always strong, motivated, and truly determined not to let that happen by any means necessary.

My family and I had had many days when things were a bit scarce, like money to pay bills, buy food or take care of other miscellaneous things. We were sometimes left with no choice but to bear our wants and needs and go without the basic essential needs. The burden of taking care of six children over the years was solely on my mother's shoulders. It wasn't easy, but she always found a way to give us a decent life.

Then one day a lady with a gentleman came knocking at my door. My sister Angelica opened the door and my mother told them to come in. The woman was dressed in a big dashiki type of dress. She was a rather large woman with fair skin. The gentleman that she was with was wearing black pants and a blue button-down shirt. He was fair skinned as well with a much slimmer build.

Anyhow the woman came inside our house with the man and introduced herself as Joyce and told my mother that she was a friend of my father's and that she knew him from Canada. She also told my mother that she too grew up in the neighbourhood and she had left to go abroad when she was a teenager. She then said that she still had family living in the area and that we might know them because some of her family knew us. Joyce had also told my mother that she had heard so many things about us and that she wanted to match our faces to the names that my father had told her. Naturally, my siblings and I introduced ourselves to her one by one until she was satisfied. So, she and my mother chatted for a while longer. The lady and the man strangely ended up spending most of their day at our house.

My mother was very warm and welcoming to our new house guests. She even offered them some of our dinner. The menu was fried chicken and white rice. So, they ate and ate and then Joyce told my mother how delicious her food was and if she could have a second serving of her delicious fried chicken. Knowing how gracious and kind my mother was, she replied yes and got Joyce her second serving of chicken. When Joyce was finished with her meal, she suggested we give her all our shoe sizes and wanted to know if we had any photographs or letters for our father that she could give him when she returned to Canada.

Talk about trusting a stranger. So, my mother agreed and told her that she would get them later before she went back abroad. Joyce thanked my mother for the meal and the gentleman, who was her brother-in-law, then left. After she left my mother asked us what we thought about Joyce. Andrea thought that she was nice and some of us didn't think much of her. Angelica and Royal thought that she was phony and a bit pretentious and very inquisitive, sort of like Miss June.

My spirit didn't take well to her, and I know that she wasn't intrigued with me either. She never struck me as a pleasant person, and she asked too many questions about my mother and father's relationship. To me, even at nine years old, there were too many signs and signals of a red flag. My mother never trusted her at all either for that matter. My mother suspected that the woman must have had an ulterior motive of some sort up her sleeve. What exactly would be in it for her to want to introduce herself and also take back to Canada our personal belongings so that she could present them to our father?

Most of all what was disappointing was that my father never made mention of this woman before or even phoned us to give a heads up and to expect visitors from Canada. But then again, he wasn't communicating with my mother. Still, he should have given her some respect where respect was due considering that my father knew my mother from when she had been a teenager and had had many children with her. They were as thick as thieves at one point or another before he left Jamaica to go to Canada. I expected more from him.

My mother had always stayed loyal to my father for as far back as I can remember. Even when many prominent businessmen were attracted to her, she never felt the same about them as they felt about her. She still stayed strong and especially loyal to my father who was thousands and thousands of miles away. At that time, I had suspected that I couldn't say the same thing about him. Some women can hold out longer than some men. Going abroad sure has a funny way of changing people, and I do mean for all the wrong reasons. My mother always thought that she knew my father very well and he knew her. She thought that he would always honour her and value her worth, but by the looks of things, he was beginning to look more and more selfish every day through my mother's lens. It was not cool with the rest of us the way he was treating her.

Joyce stayed in Jamaica for a few weeks. She came back to our house to ask my mother for permission to take my sister Andrea with her on an afternoon outing to the countryside to visit her family. So, my mother granted her permission to take her, and I think my mother was just testing her as well. Perhaps she would get answers as to who the hell this woman was to my father. Secondly, perhaps she would find out what this woman was hoping to achieve by presenting herself to us, with no warning.

In the few weeks Joyce stayed in Jamaica, the plot had already begun to thicken as she made herself available to my uncles Garth and Rupert, two scallywags. It became quite evident that they were hanging around her often and she likewise did the same. Everywhere I went I would see them together; it was almost as if my uncles were her newfound best friends. One thing that I know is that my uncles must have had something up their sleeves. They always did. And because they were never loyal to anyone, they were always in the mood for some good bribery if the price was right.

They were opportunists who would stop at nothing no matter the cost nor what was at stake as long as they got what they wanted, especially in monetary items or gifts. My mother had found out about them a long time ago when they had come from the Parish of Portland to live in Kingston. They came to live with us when my father went away to Canada and my mother naturally took them in because they were my father's brothers, and they were tired of the country life. They wanted to live and experience town life. She helped them out as much as possible with food, clothing, shelter, and how to land like a cat on their feet. She even helped them to get jobs, but those jobs didn't last very long. She soon discovered that they were lazy and always looking for the easy way out. They were selfish ingrates, and she had no respect for them after a while. Over the years they left a bad taste in her mouth, so I and my siblings barely respected them either. At that point, my mother had already asked my uncles to leave the house. I still loved my uncles and always remained polite because they were still family.

The last week before Joyce went to Canada my mother gave her the items that she requested, such as the photos, shoe print sizes, personal letters written to our father and so on. She then told my mother that she would take back all those items to my dad as soon as she reached home. In life sometimes you have to extend the olive branch, or you can simply give one the rope to hang themselves.

A few weeks later my dad had phoned my mother and told her that he had received the items that she had sent with Joyce and told my mother that she was just his good friend. My father also told my mother that he was coming back to Jamaica for a visit. He didn't know the exact date but said it would be in a few months. So, my mother was optimistic and took his word for what it was worth. She was even willing to move on with some understanding. He also told my mother that he would send her some money in the mail and that in the upcoming weeks he would send us some new shoes and clothing along with some other things in a parcel and to look out for that. So, my mother took his promised words, and in a few weeks, she did receive the parcel and the money from my father. She received fifty dollars Canadian. Fifty dollars was a lot of money at that time, and she was grateful for the help because it had been a while since my father had made mention of us or sent us anything.

When the parcel arrived, we were very excited. We became even more excited when we found out what it contained. The parcel contained some red studded leather jackets like the legendary Michael Jackson wore in his "Thriller" video. Of course, they were replicas, but we were excited to have them and were very grateful for them. We also received a lot of new clothing, toys, and new shoes for each of us. The items could not have come at a better time because we had our annual school dance coming up, and we thought that it would give us a chance to show off our new clothing, especially our new jackets.

We wore those jackets around proudly and were the talk of the town because no one else had those jackets. People had only seen the jackets in music videos and were telling us how cool we looked with them on. At the time it was as if I had an alter ego of some sort because I was really beginning to feel like a pop star myself. Yeah, go figure. Those were some memorable, exciting times in our lives. We were full of life and a ray of sunshine was beaming in on us daily, especially now that we had something else to look forward with the promised return of our father.

A few months passed, and my father kept his promise to my mother that he was coming to Jamaica to visit. He stayed true to his word, except when he came to Jamaica, he stayed with a long-time friend of his by the name of Mr. Bailey. That man was truly his best friend for life as far as I knew, even though his best friend hadn't really come to our house since my father went away to check on us to see if we were all right or if we needed anything and even though he just lived five minutes away from us. That was okay because it sometimes takes a person that is close to you to find out who is with you and who is against you. Mr. Bailey's action spoke loudly for itself. He didn't really care about my father's children; he was only a face card.

When my father came back to Jamaica, I didn't fully comprehend why he wasn't staying with us at our place like before he went away. In due time I fully understood. When my dad came to visit us for the first time in six years, he stayed outside of the gate, and he decided that he wasn't stepping a foot inside the yard. I remembered vividly that he was standing at the gate, just staring at my mother and not saying anything. It was rather an awkward scene if you can imagine, with him just standing there like a total stranger all dressed to impress and the rest of us kids wondering what was happening exactly.

As I stood there, I asked my mother why Daddy was not coming into the yard and didn't he miss us. My mother told me that she couldn't quite understand the cold stare and the negative body language that he was giving off. So, my mother and I decided that we would approach him since he wasn't coming to us. We went over to him while he was standing at the fence and my mother asked him why he was not coming inside to us. She also asked him if he was going to hug her after all this time with him being away. He told her that he wasn't going to give her any hugs or kisses, but he would certainly hug his kids, so I gave him a big hug and a kiss on his cheeks.

He also told my mother that he wasn't happy with her at all and some of the things that he had been hearing about her while he was away in Canada. My mother then said, "Things like what?" He replied that he had heard that she was seeing another man. My mother told him that was not true and asked where he had heard such a ridiculous accusation. He then turned to her and told her that his brothers Garth and Rupert had told his friend Joyce a few months prior. He said that Joyce was the one that had brought the accusation to his attention. My mother turned to my father and told him that if he had a problem with her then he should have said something to her many months ago instead of allowing lies to fester. She also told him that it was very unfair of him to no give her a chance and the benefit of the doubt to defend herself. It was obvious that he had taken sides with his brothers and a total stranger like Joyce that she didn't even know, but she remained a lady and didn't bother to get too aggressive with him or act like a fool. Things were getting awkward between them because I had never seen my parents argue before until that day. Furthermore, it wasn't the time or place to do so because people on the road were passing by and overhearing their argument which was rather uncomfortable for me.

My father told my mother that he was going to stay at Mr. Bailey's home for the rest of his stay. He also told her when he would pick up his children to visit friends and relatives with him. That was the end of it. He came for us like he said he would. I could tell that my mother was not a happy camper at all. She was devastated by his actions. He didn't even give her a chance to fight for our family. His actions and demeanour were very dismissive towards her. So much for staying loyal and dedicated. What my father did to my mother was like throwing dirt in her face. I felt her pain too. There went my once happy, caring, cordial family.

It just wasn't fair to Mother or her children at all that people, even my uncle, could make such lies that my father would foolishly fall for. It all made sense to me after a while that when Joyce had come to our house earlier, she had been up to something. She came fishing for information and not for the right reasons either. She wanted to see the real woman and mother she was matching up against. No one was surprised by my uncles' selfish, greedy actions at all. Their actions showed they were still bitter and angry and wanted revenge of some sort. They were angry at my mother because my mother had gotten rid of them. She had told them to leave her house years prior too. The question remained what was in it for Joyce and what was truly her motive.

Time passed and my father returned to Canada. One day my mother dared to confront my uncles at the same time and they both denied any involvement in the whole situation that transpired between my parents. What also transpired was my father had taken Joyce to be his new wife: my uncle told us so. Now that was some shady business that came to light. Joyce wanted my father all to herself no matter who was involved and no matter what it took. Don't get me wrong, it took two to tango and that he did, no matter the cost or consequences. My father should have had the decency to tell my mother what he was up instead of just deflecting and making it seem like she was the one that was up to no good. My father should have been more forthcoming with the truth and his decisions. Instead, my mother wasted her time all those years waiting for him to come back to her. She had somehow become a major subject of other people's gossip.

In time the truth also came out that when Joyce first came to our house and introduced herself to us as my father's friend from Canada she was already physically and emotionally invested in my father. She was already his lover. It's no wonder my mother never really trusted her. There was just something from that time that was off about her. Even then she was asking too many personal questions. My mother's impression of Joyce was that she was fake, classless, and cunning in many ways. She also left a bitter taste in my mouth. I knew that she was just a snake lurking in the gardens. Some people in this world just don't have any morals and self-respect. They want what they want by any means necessary.

A few months later I saw one of Joyce's family members. It was one of her nieces, named Jocelyn. I had known her niece a long time before her aunt had come into the picture and I gave Joyce's niece a piece of my mind, telling her exactly what I thought about her aunt. I told her that her aunt had a bad body, shaped like a camel, and that she looked like a big fat pig and that she ate like a cow. At the time I knew it wasn't the right thing for me to say, but I was only acting out in anger. I was just too involved in grown-up stuff. My issue was if a man was going to leave his woman for another one, he should make sure that she is more than the one that he left her for. Isn't that a fact?

It didn't take long for Jocelyn to tell her aunt what my true feelings were about her and exactly where my thoughts lay. I took it that the news didn't sit very well with her being abroad because I heard that she was livid. Rumor had it that she was to return to Kingston as soon as possible. I also heard that Joyce wanted to have a little chat with me. I suppose it was to give me a piece of her foreign mind. That was exactly what she did when she returned a few short months later. It didn't take her long to come to the house upon arrival. She also brought her niece as a witness to corroborate the story and her cousin Gutsy. Joyce came to my house breathing heavily and seemed hostile to a certain degree. She told my mother what I had said about her and that she didn't appreciate a little gal like me saying that about her. Then she asked my mother if she could have a word with me. The nerve of some people. There was no shame in her game.

Lee called me and asked me in front of Joyce if what she was accusing me of was true. I confirmed every word to be true, mainly because I never cared much about the whole ordeal and was never petrified of her either. What I discovered about myself at that moment in time was that there was no shame in my game either. She didn't intimidate me at all, and I got the feeling that she had sense and was not too impressed by me either. She requested that my mother discipline me by slapping me as a form of punishment. By the way, my mother wasn't having that nonsense just to suit Joyce's selfish needs. Lee always taught us to have manners with our elders and to respect others, but that day had felt like an exception to the rules. Lee never disciplined me that day. However, when Joyce left the house that day, she had a lovely chat with me to let me know that what I said many months before about Joyce wasn't very nice. I acknowledged my mistake and I moved on. The nerve of step-mommy dearest coming back to my house. I never understood why my mother never confronted her about being a phony. I guess my mother just took the high road. The right thing to do was move on.

Eventually, George and Lee became strangers to each other. A line had been drawn in the sand after a while. My parents turned from being best friends to strangers and then enemies. Life is a funny game and sometimes things in life just don't turn out as we might hope. My father being away in a foreign country did change him, and it also gave me a perspective of who he had become. My father was mostly communicating through my older sister Angelica; she became the happy medium between my parents and us. If there was something of great importance to be done, she would take charge and let both parents know. Angelica was always a very responsible and caring person; it was her character and within her nature to do so. She was always looking out for her brothers and sisters and making sure that we had our lunches and lunch money and were out the door for school in time. I truly love my sister and respect her for that.

CHAPTER 8

Immigrating to Canada

I had often wondered when that day would come for me to be with my father in Canada. My imagination conjured up bright lights, a big city, and no more poverty, killings nor suppression by others around me. My initial thoughts led me to believe that in Canada there was an entirely different world of peace, and it would be a lot different from the world that I grew up in. I thought that it would be a country of peace, love, unity, and without violence. It was told to me that it was a place to aim high and to reach for the impossible dreams because the sky would be the limit. I just wanted a change of scenery and a different environment to grow up in because I was getting older and wiser. Maturity was setting in and I had a better understanding of things and my surroundings.

I didn't try to get between my parents' problems and indifferences because they were both equally important to me. I tried not to choose sides. I also didn't mind the fact that Joyce was my stepmother and the possibility of me living with her and my father abroad didn't bother me at all. In fact, I had gotten used to the idea for quite some time. Like I said, I was more mature, headstrong, and was looking at the bigger picture of going far away to be with my father on a plane, far away in a new country. How very fortunate for me to have that to look forward to.

Some time earlier, my father had filed with Immigration Canada for us to immigrate to Canada. My mother finally got word that it was time for us to gather and prepare ourselves to leave Jamaica. The news had come sooner than she had expected, and we had to move fast to gather ourselves and line up all our ducks in a row. We were told by our mother not to tell a soul and not to share the information of our good news with anyone. She didn't trust that many people and she was uneasy about our safety and bad-minded people. That's just the way it was in the ghetto. Not everyone was going to embrace your good news and be happy for you. As far as my mother was concerned, some of them were like crabs in a bucket. She had seen too many pokers faces too many times to make that kind of mistake.

We were only allowed to tell our teachers and make them know ahead of time that we weren't coming back to school. I was going to miss my closest friends because they were special to me. My friends had shown me love and kindness and had been very empathic to me over the years. I really appreciated all of them for that. It was hard for me knowing that I couldn't make mention of the good news to my friends. So, I disobeyed my mother's order and I told some of my close friends' days before that I was leaving them to go away to Canada and I didn't know when I was coming back. My friends and I spoke, and we told each other how much we would miss each other. We promised to write to one another soon.

In wintry December my father sent for four of his children, including me, Angelica, Andrea and Ian. Of course, Audley and Royal were left behind. They couldn't travel with us since they were not my father's biological children. Who would have thought? My father always showed them unconditional love and treated them like his own. The situation was quite unfortunate for Audley and Royal that I was going to be separated from them and that they would not share the same fate as me or have the experience with us travelling on a plane. It saddened me terribly. It was as if someone had cut off my right arm and I was only left with one, just helpless.

From time to time I began to analyze the situation that presented itself to me and I tried to focus on the positives for we didn't know what the future might hold for Audley and Royal. Perhaps it was a blessing in disguise that they stayed behind to cater to our mother and attend to her emotional needs. Besides, it wouldn't have been a great feeling knowing that my mother was all alone in Jamaica herself. Don't get me wrong, everyone deserves an equal opportunity to spread their wings and fly, However, I must admit perhaps it was a bit selfish on my part. When I look on the bright side, I think my mother would be a bit lonely and lost if everyone had left her all at once.

My mother was told by my father that we should not bring any clothing or any of our items. He said we should travel light and not with many things because he had already spent a lot of money for new items for us and that he and his wife had prepared everything already for us. We were excited and remained optimistic about that.

We boarded the plane at Norman Manley International Airport with only one carry-on bag among us and headed straight to Canada. While my siblings and I were on the plane we were very observant about everything on that Air Canada flight, including what the flight attendants were wearing. They were polite and very nice to us I must say. We were also observing the passengers that surrounded us and most of all the interior structure of the plane. We were terrified and everything was so new to us. We had never been on a plane before in our lives, only in my dreams.

So, we waited in anticipation not knowing what to expect. All sorts of notions were going through my head about how long I would be on the plane sitting before it landed. When I finally reached the foreign land, my hope was just to reach our destination safely in one piece. I just remember having moments of silence and prayer until we finally reached our destination in Canada. Just before the plane landed, I recall seeing a lot of light below. I had never seen so many lights in my entire life, and my sisters and brother began to get excited because we knew that we were flying over the Canadian skies.

When we landed and came off the plane it took us a while for customs to sort us because we were young children, and we were new to the country. It took some time, but we made it out of there in one piece. It didn't take long for our father to recognize us and give us a big hug. He had travelled to the airport alone; Joyce wasn't with him that day and none of us ever bothered asking him about her either.

My father gathered us and led us to where he had parked his car. Then he loaded the one little carry-on bag into the trunk, and we drove to our new home. On our way there, my father asked us if we had enjoyed our flight and we replied and told him, "Yes, indeed, very much so." So, we continued to drive and trod along to our new home. It took my father about twenty minutes to get home from Pearson International airport in Toronto. All I kept thinking about were bright lights in a big city and could this be real, could someone please pinch me and wake me up. For this was certainly a dream come true and with the conclusion that I had finally arrived at our new life.

My father pulled up beside a house and parked on the side of the street and told us that we were here at our new home and that we could get out of the car. Then my father opened the trunk and took out what little luggage we had arrived with to this new country of ours. He told us to follow him inside the house, and so we did. When we arrived inside, I saw my father's wife sitting in the living room on the couch with two small children and her older daughter, Claudia.

We entered the front entrance of the living room and I and my siblings politely said to the lady of the house good night and the lady of the house replied to good night in a dry tone. She didn't exactly greet us in a warm, fuzzy, welcoming manner. The feeling was a bit awkward, but we still made a conscious effort to say hello and took the initiative to give her a hug one by one because my mother raised us to always be polite. We all stood there staring at each other. Frankly it was getting more awkward and uncomfortable by the minute. My father tried to interact with everyone and make small chat, sort of trying to break the ice.

We continued standing there in silence while the lady of the house silently sat there on the couch. It was not quite the reaction or welcome that we were expecting, but then again, we didn't have much expectation of her either. We were hoping that all would be well. Then my father started asking us questions about our flight again. He was sort of trying to stir the sudden stillness because if a needle had fallen, we would have been able to hear it. Then Joyce began to engage in the conversation and asked us how we were doing and if we were all right. We replied and told her that we were fine, thank you, because we were taught by our mother to always have manners and to be polite. Then my older sister Angelica told my father that we were hungry and that we barely ate the food on the flight because it wasn't tasty at all but rather odd. Perhaps we just were not used to chicken, or beef prepared in that manner. I supposed it would take us a while to get used to the food and the culture.

Then my father told us that dinner was in the kitchen and that he would share some food with us and that my siblings and I should join him in the kitchen. In the meantime, Joyce showed us to our quarters and where we would be sleeping. She took us upstairs and her young children followed suit. She showed us around and where to find the bathroom and so forth. Then she took us to the bedroom where we were going to sleep. It was a small room painted blue with two single beds on each side. It had a very large window panel and the trim was painted white.

She then told us that we would have to share the room and that the room originally belonged to her two smallest children, Monique and Colleen, and that my sister Andrea would share a room with her eldest daughter, Claudia. Andrea was glad to comply or maybe just relieved that she didn't have to crumple up like a sardine in a tin. Of course, I didn't mind at all, because I was used to bunking with my siblings in Jamaica. I could gladly share a room with them in Canada. I was glad to finally be with my father and the rest of my family.

We were in one of the rooms upstairs and Joyce's room was right next to ours and she had knocked on our door to give us a tour of the house and we followed her around. Then she showed us downstairs where the basement was. At first, when Joyce made mention of a basement, I did not have any idea what a basement was. Then I asked her, and she told me it was downstairs at the bottom of the house. We followed her and went down to the basement. It was very cold with lots of open space with a loveseat and a television on a silver chrome and glass television stand. It looked all right with a small brown area rug over the concrete cold floor. Joyce told us that the basement is where we would be spending most of the day and the room upstairs was for sleeping purposes at night. Joyce didn't waste any time laying down the house rules.

There was a total of nine of us living in that three-bedroom house and a basement. Three children belong to Joyce and four of us were my father's children. I totally understood that we were in a new space and a different environment. I knew that it was going to take some time for everyone to get to know each other and for us to make any adjustments needed with my newfound blended family. And we came to find out that night that Joyce's youngest daughter, Monique, was my father's biological daughter. So that made her my little sister as well. That was too much information for me to process in one night. A part of me knew it was going to be difficult, but I was optimistic that it would work. By the end of the night, we finally had something to eat. We were famished after such a long day. We were very much exhausted, so we went to bed and looked forward to the next day and our new beginning.

Our First Christmas in Canada

A cold chill that filled the air and a lot of snow had fallen to the ground the evening before, which was a pretty good indication that winter had arrived. It was a week before Christmas and school was already out for the winter holiday break. Everyone was at home at the same time except for my father. He was always at work working hard to provide for his family.

A few weeks had passed since my siblings, and I had arrived in this new country. We were still fresh off the boat or in this case fresh off the plane. It was a slow process for us and getting used to our new life and the cold temperature that came along with it. Lord knows that it wasn't as easy transitioning as I would've hoped for while being around my new family. As I was still fresh in the place after a few weeks I noticed that my stepsisters addressed my father as Daddy! At first, I didn't quite understand why Claudia and Colleen would call my father Daddy, since my little sister Monique was his only biological child that he had with my stepmother. To be frank, I didn't find it cute or endearing at all that they called him Daddy. It was a bit confusing to me as well as my siblings. Oh well, welcome to the new normal I guess, but I merely wished someone had given me the memo beforehand. Nevertheless, we would soon find out.

At first, I thought that they were having conversations about their fathers since all three of them had three different fathers. Monique was the youngest of my father's biological children, so she was related to me. She was the child that Joyce and my father had shared. Yep, that was my little sister. That was cool with me. I didn't mind at all that I had the big sister role again. I was already playing big sister to my little brother Ian, so I didn't mind at all. I was used to that role by now.

I let my curiosity and emotions get the best of me, and I asked my stepmother's eldest daughter, Claudia, why she call my father Daddy. I was just hoping to clear up any confusion that I had, but I don't think she took well to the question because she aggressively replied that if my father didn't have a problem with her calling him Daddy, then neither should I. Well, I told her that he wasn't her father and that she needed to go and find her own. I guess in a way she was right, and it was petty of me and perhaps somewhat presumptuous of me to think that others should not address my father as Daddy. I was not trying to be a poop disturber or anything like that. I was just curious and perhaps a little jealous to share my father with the rest of them. Besides, I was still trying to get used to certain things. I asked myself why I should let that bother me the slightest bit. I guessed I would have to get used to that sooner than later.

So that evening Joyce decided to take us to the Albion Mall. She took two of her children, Claudia and Colleen, along with my sister Andrea and me. My eldest sister declined to go to the mall with us. She was not too intrigued or in the mood for a small trip because it was not like Joyce was going to spend any money and buy us anything anyway. I understood that it wasn't her job or anything like that to buy anything for us. It was my father's responsibility for us being in this country, after all. It was not like my stepmother owed us anything at all. But I could say that she might have been a little bit or partly responsible for us; we were not responsible for ourselves!

Whenever we went to the mall with her, she never got us anything at all, no matter how small or little the amount was for the items. I would like to think I'm not the ungrateful type. It was not in her character to do so, but from time to time she would only buy my sister Andrea some things. I guess she took a liking to her even in Jamaica. Joyce always thought that Andrea resembled my father more than the rest of us. I still wanted to go anyway because going to the mall was better than staying at home, which would be too boring. I had not been to many places in the short time that I had been in Canada, just mainly to school and back.

We went to the mall and Joyce proceeded to her favourite department store. That was the only store she had ever taken me to apart from her second favourite store. We decided to look around the store at all sorts of things, from clothing to appliances to Christmas items and decorations. While we were in the Christmas decoration department my sister Andrea saw a piece of garbage from the floor. It looked like a piece of tassel that probably fell from one of the Christmas trees that were on display. Andrea picked up the shiny blue tassel and was walking around the department store with it all evening long.

Anyhow we left the department store. Joyce didn't purchase anything for herself or her children that day and we headed straight home. That evening we waited for my father to get home as usual and when he arrived, we greeted him with a hug as we normally did. About ten minutes later, my stepmother summoned me to come to the living room. When I came and sat in the living room Joyce concocted a story and told my father that I had stolen Christmas decorations from the Kmart department store. I was totally shocked and so were my sisters Andrea and Angelica and my brother Ian. I told my father that I did not steal anything, and I would not do that because I was not a thief. I even told my father that it was my sister Andrea that had picked up a piece of rubbish tassel from Kmart.

I was very angry that Joyce had lied about and said that about me for I did no such thing. Furthermore, I would never attempt to do something like that. If I had never done that when I was in Jamaica, why would I do that now that I was in Canada? My father asked me if I did what Joyce was accusing me of and I told him I never did. He was very irate and upset with me, even though I was telling him that I didn't do anything wrong. But he wasn't listening to me or my truth and to what I was saying to him. He wanted to believe what he wanted to believe and that hurt my feelings to the core. Lord knows I wasn't lying, and my sister Andrea didn't step up to the plate and take responsibility for the rubbish either. She just left me hanging on a limb all by myself. Joyce knew it was trash too and with her false accusation, the question remained as to why? Besides, what did I have to gain by picking up garbage from a store? Joyce was really beginning to show who she really was. It became evident that the women clearly did not like me at all.

Second, if I had stolen something from Kmart, why didn't Joyce make mention of the whole fiasco at the time it happened? Why was this being the first time that she had made mention of it? My father was angry and the next thing you know he started cursing me out like never before. I have never seen my father that pissed off before in all my life. He told me that he had expected better things from me than this. The next thing I knew, he slapped me in the face. I was utterly disgusted by his actions because in no way, shape or form did I deserve that slap. Not today, not tomorrow, not ever. Then I started crying that my father had never hit me a day in his life. I was very upset, hurt, and pissed off for I knew in my heart of hearts that I did nothing wrong and never deserved that kind of treatment from anyone.

Then the next thing that I knew Joyce was telling my father that I had told her daughter Claudia that I said that she should not call him Daddy because he was not her father. Talk about adding a whole gasoline tank to the fire and adding insult to injuries. The smirk on my stepmother's face was haunting. She looked quite cold and calculated, not to mention very mischievous. The whole situation reminded me of the past and brought back old feelings of her in Jamaica a few years prior when I had met Joyce for the first time.

You see, a leopard never changes her spots no matter how much you shave off its hair.

My spirit was dampened; I began feeling down but not out for some odd reason, so I decided that I would go to bed early. I decided that would be the best remedy for me that evening. About half an hour later Angelica and Ian came upstairs. After I reasoned with them both and told them what had just happened from my viewpoint, then my sister consoled me and told me that it was going to be all right. The pep talk helped tremendously because it gave me back my confidence and reassurance that I would be fine once this ordeal was put behind me. Or at least that is what I had hoped.

The next morning Joyce gathered us to say that Angelica, Andrea, Ian, and I would from then on be staying in the basement of the house. She said to gather our belongings and make our way to the basement because that was where we would be staying from now on. She also said that the reason for the decision was that her children needed to have back their room from now on. She also said that the children were constantly complaining about how much they missed their rooms, and they didn't feel the need to share a room with us anymore.

Without hesitation, we told her okay and then started packing up the few belongings that we had and went down to the basement. It never took us very long to pack and gather our things because as per my father's request, we didn't come to Canada with many items anyhow. He had told us that we must not worry about anything because he had gotten all that taken care of and that he and his wife had already gone shopping to purchase new clothing for us. My father assured us that he had it all figured out. But from the looks of things, he hadn't figured out much because we still didn't have much clothing, just the little that we came to this country with. And we had left a lot of good quality clothing back home. The only clothing that we had ever received from Joyce came from thrift stores. Whenever Joyce went to the thrift stores, she would come back with quite a few second-hand items, such as winter jackets, fur coats, pants, sweaters, and so forth. As soon as she would get home, she would start to talk and elaborate about all the lovely items that she had purchased and how expensive they were and how much money she had spent on everything. I could give someone a quarter for each time that she made that statement as if we were stupid. We knew it was second-hand clothing she got and expected us to wear. We were not used that kind of thing, but we would soon get used to it because we had no choice. I mean, we couldn't exactly walk around naked and freeze our butts off.

We went to the basement as requested by our stepmother. I was never the disobedient or the defiant type, so I did what I was told with urgency. The basement as you can imagine wasn't the best room in the house. It was cold, lonely, and dingy. It was dingy in the sense that it was dull. It lacked brightness to the walls as not much sunlight could come in down there. Also, the mainly old unwanted furniture loomed in the basement. It was lacking the comfort aspect in more ways than one. Even though the basement was cold most of the time I eventually got used to it. The basement after a while brought me a little peace and solitude at night, especially when everyone was sleeping.

My siblings and I did the best we could to make the basement our home. We tried to make our stay as comfortable as possible. It was as if we were confined to the basement, and we had to spend most of our time in that part of the house. Christmas would eventually come that year and I began to miss my mother dearly. I couldn't quite understand why we were not hearing from our mother at all. Even when my older sister Angelica had written to her regularly, we hadn't heard anything from her for a while, not even a phone call. That was very odd considering that we used to communicate with her very regularly. It seemed to be getting less and less as the days went by. Besides, it was the holiday season, and I was starting to feel a bit uneasy. One evening when my stepmother wasn't there, it was just my father with us at home. I told my father that I hadn't heard anything from my mother and that I was worried. I asked if he could give her a phone call for us so that we could say hello.

My father agreed to the terms and dialled up my mother. She was very happy and delighted to hear from us and so was I. Hearing her voice for such a long time brought me some relief to know that everything was okay. Then my sister Angelica asked my mother if she had received the letters that she had written to her, and my mother told her yes. Then my mother asked Angelica if she had received the letters that my mother had written to us, and Angelica had told her no. We hadn't received any such letters. I'm pretty sure that the mail carriers were not on strike. My mother reassured us that she was writing to us regularly. My mother also mentioned that she called us sometimes, but Joyce always told her that she was on the other phone line, and she would let us know that she had called. But of course, she didn't tell us anything, and we certainly weren't receiving any of our mother's written letters either.

We hurried up the conversation before Joyce came home and told my mother that we would stay in touch. I told my father thanks for the phone call, and we were feeling much better. I was feeling much better on the outside but not too much on the inside for whenever we had asked Joyce if our mother had called, she assured us that she hadn't. Those actions were bizarre and confusing. I had quickly discovered how cunning my stepmother truly was, for I knew in my heart that she was out to get us. She didn't like us much, especially me. Actions always speak louder than words and her actions showed that she was not for us. She only loved the bull not the calves.

As the weeks and months passed by, Joyce gave me and sister Angelica and my brother Ian all the household chores to do—not so much my sister Andrea. I think she like Andrea more than the rest of us, and Joyce was also trying to drive a wedge between the rest of us. She would hardly give Andrea any household chores to do, and Joyce would take her with them when they were going places. Joyce didn't give any of her children any chores to do at all. It was always us doing the bathroom, cleaning the dishes, wiping the floors, every single day that went by. After all, Joyce told us about a few months in, "I didn't send for you to come to Canada to have a good time. I sent for you to work." Those were her exact words and something that would never be forgotten. She worked us day and night like her slaves. She even turned my sister Angelica into her hairdresser for her children. She would always boss around my sister to comb her children's hair multiple times a week, every week. She would also rudely push her around to help her children with their homework daily as well. Every day Joyce would always make sure that we stayed busy. Most of the days my father wasn't at home to witness her ill-treatment and the ill will she had for us. However, when we would explain our hurt and our position, he would minimize the situation and try to keep the peace as much as possible.

CHAPTER 10

Fifty Shades of Disagreements and Abuse

A few years had passed, and my stepmother had tried everything to get on my last nerves. Everywhere I turned she was always giving me chores to do, picking a fight, or making up some fabricated unconscionable lies about me.

One day I had wiped out the whole household from top to bottom. Joyce then went outside, got an old ice cream bucket and filled it with dirt, brought it back inside, and sprinkled it all over the floors from top to bottom. She looked at me angrily and said, "Clean this house again because it is not done properly." That got me really upset and I told her that she didn't need to do that. It was not necessary. Joyce then turned to me and slapped me in my face. Tears started to flow from my eyes down to my cheeks. On top of that, I had to clean the stupid house again. If she had a magic wand to wave so that I could just disappear and not ever exist, then she would have done so.

From there on after Joyce had some new rules that she wanted to lay down for her stepchildren. She once again summoned us to the living room for a house meeting. She told us that we were not allowed to sit in the living room, especially on her couches, because the living room was off-limits to us. It was strictly for her and her kids and her guests. She always made it clear that we were not allowed to use her telephone to make any phone calls, not even to phone our mother. She also made it clear that we were not allowed to enter upstairs. We were not allowed in any of the rooms up there for that matter. She would also hide the snacks in the bedroom for her and her kids after she went grocery shopping. She also said that we were only to enter upstairs for the sole purpose of using the bathroom, because there was one bathroom in the house, and it was unfortunately upstairs. She also told us that we should always make sure that the house was kept clean just in case her relatives stopped by, especially her favourite aunt, Aunty Blanch. When her Aunty Blanch visited, they would chat and gossip about us like dogs as if we weren't present or couldn't hear every word that they were saying about us. Joyce's final words that day were that we should never call her Joyce and that we should address her by calling her Mrs. Shepherd for that was the name by marriage. I thought that was ridiculous, but that's who she was, a total narcissistic drama queen. Well, the last time I checked we were Shepherds too, born and bred.

What's next? I thought. I felt as if she didn't want us around and she wanted to annihilate us as far as I was concerned—except for my sister Andrea. Joyce must have really liked Andrea ever since we were in Jamaica because she never gave her any chores to do, and Andrea never seemed to have the rest of our backs. Maybe it was because she had become best friends with Joyce's oldest daughter, Claudette, and completely abandoned us. I couldn't quite understand it, and it was beginning to leave a sour taste in my mouth.

We abided by my stepmother's rules for a while. I felt as if I were Cinderella in a bad *Twilight Zone* series. My stepmother didn't seem to make my life any easier daily. She enjoyed being a ruthless shit disturber! Whenever she thought that the dishes were not done properly, she would tell us to do them over and over until she was satisfied. My stepmother's behaviour was becoming increasingly erratic as the weeks and months and years went by—so erratic that one day she told me that she was having visitors come over and that I needed to sweep and wipe out the living room. I often wondered why I had to always clean the living room. It was not like I was allowed to sit in there anyway. I always thought that it was tacky that I was only allowed in there for strictly cleaning purposes. But as my stepmother would remind us from time to time, the only reason they sent us from Jamaica was to work and to be her footstool.

Doing what I was told, I began to dust off the marble coffee table. That was her pride and joy. How she just so adored vanity. Then I began sweeping the hardwood floor. The next step was to mop and thoroughly polish the floors. When I was still perfecting the floor, Joyce started complaining that the floor was not cleaned properly and was implying that I had missed many spots. I thought the floor looked pretty good from where I was standing. But it seems to me that my stepmother was very dissatisfied with my work. The next thing I knew Joyce stormed through the front door and came back a few minutes later with a container filled with dirt. She started cursing like a sailor, then she started pouring out the dirt all over the floor that I had just polished. I was angry but not surprised. But for the life of me, I didn't understand what the hell was wrong with her. From then on, as I was getting older and much wiser, I knew that she had to have been crazy and mentally disturbed. It was either that or her contempt for me was seeping through her pores. I also learned that misery loves company; she was starting to get inside of my head and was testing my patience and faith. It was wearing me down.

I was trying my hardest at times to be on my best behaviour and other times I didn't really care. Furthermore, it had become increasingly difficult with her antagonizing immature behaviour. I was not used to anyone pushing me around and with such vile ignorance attached to it. Not even back home in the concrete jungles of Jamaica did I get treated like that. Sometimes I considered that it would have been better for me if I had just stayed with my mother in Jamaica. Being in a foreign country was not what I expected by any stretch of my imagination. The only solution was to stay humble and bite my tongue. I didn't want any more problems because everywhere I turned in that household controversy followed me. It seemed inevitable though, for Joyce wasn't rational or even receptive to reasoning. It was her way or the highway. She made sure of that. She was an overgrown, immature bully and many of her friends and relatives were intimidated by her.

Joyce had a friend by the name of Neeni and a first cousin named Gutsy who were visiting Canada from Jamaica on a visitor visa. They both wanted to make a new life in Canada, so they decided not to go back home. They had jobs working under the table and they lived with us for a short while. Joyce called Immigration Services on them one day to say that her friend and cousin were in Canada illegally. She just wanted to control every aspect of their lives and she had somehow lost control. She also wanted half of their paycheques as well. A chatty mouth cousin of Joyce told Neeni and Gutsy what was happening and what Joyce had done. When Immigration came to pick them up, they weren't home. They had run away and never returned. As for me, I wasn't intimidated one bit by her evil presence even though she had become unpredictable. I believed in prayer and knew that one day the Lord would deliver me out of the lion's den.

It was a Wednesday evening and my stepmother called me to come up from the basement and join her in the living room. Wow, I said to myself, Joyce asked me to sit in the living room? I am pretty sure that hell hasn't frozen over. It's either that or she must be up to something. Well, I sat down with Joyce and Claudette, her eldest daughter, and Colleen, who was her middle child. When I sat down, Joyce began telling me that I did not resemble anyone in my family, except for my mother except for my mother, whom I resembled a lot. She then looked at me in all seriousness and said to me that she didn't feel that I was my father's child. I asked her what she mean by that. She then said to me, "I think that you are a jacket." Well, in Jamaica when someone says that to a person, it simply means that they are not legitimate. Someone else must be the daddy. Also, it would mean that my mother must have been promiscuous and that someone else might be my father instead of George Shepherd.

Well, when she said that her daughter began laughing. Apparently, I was the butt of their joke. I was the laughingstock. I was not laughing because I didn't find it funny at all. It was rather appalling, degrading, and insulting to me and my mother's character—my father's character too. I didn't like what she said to me because I knew that she gone too far. But that was Joyce for you. She had no limits, care or regard for anyone, especially me. Stigma took me over that day, perhaps to the point of no return for me. When Joyce said that to me, I felt shame and embarrassment almost as if something was wrong with me. Even though I knew within myself that it wasn't true at all, I couldn't stop thinking, what if it was true? This type of treatment saddened me deeply. Unhappiness had somehow begun to take over my soul because Joyce's bad behaviour was happening more and more regularly. That was a low point in my life, and my confidence was beginning to break down slowly but surely. I didn't know how to handle certain situations, and I had somehow needed my father to fight some of these unwanted battles for me. But he was always missing in action. He was either too busy with work or something or other. Even when he was around, he didn't put Joyce in her rightful place and set the record straight. It was as if his hands were tied behind his back and the wool had been pulled over his eyes. It sure felt as if he were castrated ninety-nine percent of the time.

It was all starting to be too much for me. Most of the time I would be in the basement just sobbing to myself. My older sister Angelica had gotten a job and she wasn't around as much anymore. I would only see her in the mornings before school and she usually came home at night after work when I was sleeping. I felt as if I couldn't turn to my father, because he wasn't advocating for us as much anymore about the way we were being treated. He was always hard working and wasn't really about the drama. Most of the time he just wanted some peace and quiet, and he was tired of his wife always complaining about his children. That made him miserable and very confused most of the time.

One weekend when my father was at home and Joyce and the rest of her children were away it gave me some home alone time with my father to bond and watch sports together. He was a big sports fan and he taught me everything there was to know about baseball and tennis. It was like he had a sports encyclopedia inside his brain. I gathered enough courage and expressed to my father that day that I wasn't happy inside the house and with all the negativity and abuse that was going on. I also shared my thoughts that Canada wasn't as cracked up to be as I had expected. I also expressed my concerns to him that I thought that his wife was picking on me for a fight a lot. He told me to try my hardest and to not pay her any mind. Whenever there was a problem that was always his reply: "Don't bother to pay Joyce any mind." It was easy for him to say, but it was becoming very hard for me to do, because whoever feels it knows it.

I didn't want to crack like an egg under pressure and stress in my young life. I knew if I had cracked under pressure, it would have given my stepmother ammunition to justify her rotten behaviour. At that point in my life, I had to tell my father that Joyce had called me a "jacket" and that discussion didn't sit well with my father at all. I thought that he had the right to know what his wife was saying to me and the rest of his children. I wasn't trying to be mischievous at all. I was only updating him and keeping him informed on a need-to-know basis. Too many things had been going on inside the household, and I was just making sure that he knew what kind of stress we were going through with his wife, Mrs. Shepherd as she would like to be called.

If it wasn't one thing, then it was another. My sister Angelica worked at Wool-co department store. I was very happy for her because it gave her a chance for independence and to see what was happening in the outside world. She seemed much happier as well. It also gave me a chance to learn about places and to hear stories of everyday people and their work life. That was interesting compared to my boring life being cooped up in a basement and doing chores all the time. The only time I felt free, alive, and stress-free was when I was at middle school.

Anyhow, Angelica was always working hard, and she made sure that she took care of us and bought things for us. Whether it was underwear or a new shirt or dress, she would always spend on us just like my mother would. There was nothing that she wouldn't do for us, and I really appreciated that. My brother and sister appreciated that too. At least she gave us a chance to wear real clothing apart from thrift store stuff.

One night when Angelica came home, I heard a quarrel that woke me up, so I got up and I saw Joyce arguing with my sister. She must have waited for my sister to come home. Joyce was telling my sister Angelica that she needed to start giving her half of her paycheque so she could pay the utility bill. My sister didn't look pleased or thrilled at all; she was ambushed. It was evident by the look that she had on her face.

Joyce was yelling at her and was extremely rude. It was not one of her finest moments or any other moment for that matter. It had become apparent that she was being a bossy bully. Joyce insisted that my sister agree to her terms to hand over half her paycheque. You see Joyce appeared to be fundamentally manipulative and a cantankerous woman. She would never stop until she made life difficult for everyone else. I mean, who argues with someone in the middle of the night about someone else's money? Could it not have been resolved another time or another day like civilized people would do? For the sake of not prolonging an argument, my sister agreed to her terms. Then our stepmother left and went back upstairs to her quarters. I could tell by the look on my sister's face that she was not happy or impressed after that altercation.

Angelica was complaining to the rest of us that she didn't think that the situation was fair because she had to work so hard while going to school to make a dollar, and now she had to give half of it to Joyce. I thought that was not cool at all. My sister should give Joyce some money but not half of her paycheque. Angelica was also worried that she might not have enough money to continue to buy us nice things anymore. Talk about a teenager being stressed out. I began feeling sorry for my sister. Her pain became my pain, especially knowing that she was only trying to make things better for her sisters and brother.

As time went by, we had to learn how to be strong and get tougher and take it all in stride, especially when Joyce's Aunty Blanch would come over on the weekend. I dreaded the times when she would visit the house on the weekends. Blanch was most unkind to me and my sisters. While she visited, she and her niece would sit in the living room or the kitchen and gossip about me, my mother, and my siblings non-stop while we were present. Whether we happened to be amid them doing some chores or passing by randomly, they would take great pleasure and delight in slaughtering us like pigs. They would paint us in the most negative light, talking about how we didn't have any manners and how much they couldn't stand us or our mother. Joyce would also rant about how no child, or their mother was going to break up a marriage and that my mother wasn't going to take her husband away from her. She was obviously a very insecure person and had low self-esteem.

One evening I was in the basement with Angelica, and Joyce came down and told me to go upstairs and do the dishes. I was still conversing with my sister, and I didn't move fast enough for Joyce, so she reached out and stabbed me on my right shoulder with a long kitchen fork. The stab was so deep that blood began to gush up, and I was bleeding profusely. The pain that I felt that day was excruciating. I began to scream, cry and yell at Joyce in a rage. My sister Angelica was crying and in shock as she had to witness my stepmother assault me like that. Angelica was helpless and couldn't do anything to save me that evening. When my daddy came home that night he argued with Joyce and tried to set her straight about her action, but she didn't care. Her behaviour was escalating and becoming worse and worse over the years.

One day Joyce slapped Angelica in the face and accused her of stealing jewelry out of her room, while Joyce was vacationing in Jamaica with my father and her two young children. Angelica pleaded with Joyce that day and told her that she did not steal anything from her and that she wasn't a thief—never had been and never would be. We all knew that she did not commit such a disgraceful act. Little did Joyce know that her older daughter Claudia had had her two besties staying in her mother's room. While they were away, Claudia and her friend were in and out of that room as if they were running a hotel room. Even though my sister Angelica had known that she still never ratted out Claudia. While it was all happening her children and the rest were just watching as it was all unfolding in front of us. Joyce kicked my sister out of the house that evening and her best friend Jacklyn came to pick her up. The weird part about the whole situation was as Anjelica was about to step foot through the door. Joyce called out to her and then said to her that she had found the ring that I was looking for. She didn't even apologize for her mistake of accusing my sister of theft, anyhow my sister kept it moving and went too live with Jacklyn and her parents.

After a while, it was me, Ian and Andrea living in the house with Joyce and the rest of her children. Andrea would eventually run away one day because my father received a phone call from her high school. The teacher stated that Andrea had not shown up for classes in three weeks. It turns out that she was skipping school along with my stepsister Claudia. My father was really pissed off to hear such distressing news, so he eventually put an ass whooping on her.

Andrea packed a garbage bag of clothes and ran away that night and never returned.

I was now left in the house with my brother Ian to face the music alone. The abuse got worse and worse. Our only escape was to play sports. We joined the basketball and track and field teams at our schools. Even though we went to different schools, the goal was still the same: to be competitive, work hard, and win. I started taking trips across Ontario to play basketball and excelled in track and field. I went to the Ontario Federation of School Athletics (OFSAA) four years in a row throughout my high school years. I enjoyed going to OFSAA because I got to get away from my abusive home, stay in hotels and get paid twenty-five dollars per day for three days usually. Joyce wasn't a happy camper about it. She was jealous and annoyed with my accomplishments, for she could not take my talents away from me while her children lay around like lazy sacks of potatoes.

The only thing that her children knew how to be was problematic and mischievous, just like their mama. In fact, one day their same chatty mouth cousin said that my stepsisters would sometimes put bleach in my shampoo and conditioner. I wasn't shocked or surprised one bit of that disturbing news. That explains why they were always laughing and whispering amount themselves each time, I was washing my hair. It all began to make so much sense to me as to the reasons why my shampoo and conditioner smelled so foul and my eyeballs where on fired after every use. There wasn't much I could do about the situation or confront them about it. I immediately discontinue the use of the products.

One Saturday I was hanging out with two of my besties down the street from where I lived. I left to go back home for something and told them that I would be in a few minutes. When I entered the house that day, my stepmother attacked me in the doorway. She told me that I had been gone all day and that I hadn't done any chores. She approached me and started hitting, punching, kicking, and slapping me. That day I found the strength inside of me to push her away from me. My stepmother then went outside and got a tall piece of metal pipe and came back inside the house and hit me on my arm with it. I ran out of the house as if I were running for my life. I ran back down the street to my friend's house, and I called the police. The ambulance came and drove me to the hospital. My arm began to swell, and I was feeling a type of pain like no other. I was sure my arm was broken. When I got to the hospital the doctor asked me what had happened, and I told him what my stepmother had done. The doctor ran some tests, but my arm was not broken. It was badly sprained and bruised up and then he wrapped it up in a sling.

Within the hour I saw my father show up at the hospital. He then told me that when the police came in to question me that I should minimize the situation and tell the police that Joyce didn't do it. He then made up a story and told me to tell the police that I fell. Well, eventually the police came, but they spoke to the doctors, my father, and they never questioned me. So, I don't know what was said and there was no arrest made.

When I left the hospital, I ended up staying with my best friend, Antoinette, down the street for two weeks. The whole time I was at her house I dreaded going home. Eventually, the day would come when I had to go back home. My stepmother told my father that she needed an apology from me to be let back inside of the home. I told my father that I was the only victim, and I should not have to apologize for someone else's disgusting, cruel behaviour.

I told him that I wouldn't do it, but eventually, I did. Can you imagine apologizing for the pain and hurt that someone else inflicted on you? That was so humiliating for me. A few weeks later I was kicked out of the house and my older brother Audley, who was now residing in Canada, came and got me. Audley and Angelica rented a home and I lived with them. So, my younger brother was left in the house with Joyce to handle and cope with her abusive, manic behaviour.

After I moved, my father and stepmother bought a house together and they moved with their younger children and my brother Ian. Ian didn't fair well on his own. He had difficulties with the law over the years.

My father eventually had an affair with another woman and divorced my stepmother. During the divorce decree, my father told his lawyer that he didn't want anything from the assets that they owned together. He walked away with nothing, even though his lawyer asked him over and over if he was sure about what he wanted.

My stepmother later died of cancer and I along with my siblings went to her funeral. But before she died, she called me on a three-way call with my younger sister Monique. Joyce wanted to talk further about the woman that my father was with and her dislike for the woman. How ironic, but for the life of me I couldn't understand why on God's green earth she wanted to speak with me. During this time Joyce was having difficulties talking and breathing because she was using an oxygen mask. The cancer had gotten bad for her, and I was feeling sorry for her in a sense. I wouldn't wish cancer or death on anyone, not even my worst enemies. Perhaps she wanted to clear her conscience before she passed.

Life is about finding peace and forgiveness for others even when they have wronged you and persecuted you without a cause. Hatred will spread inside you and before you know it, it will eat and rot away at your living soul. Sometimes victims of abuse never fully recover, and the memories live inside of my mind and thoughts. All I can do is cope and think about positive things because there is always someone else out there that is going through something far worse. Even when people try to break you and crush your soul, you must not let them do so, by being like them. Always try to be the best of you that you can be because the best is yet to come.

Whenever it pours it rains. Even when the rain is pouring down hard and doesn't seem to be letting up, it cannot and will not rain forever. The sun comes out even if it might not seem as bright at the beginning. But a brighter and greater sun always comes out to shine after a storm. A greater and brighter day always comes even though you might not recognize it at first. You must always remember that the sun doesn't just shine just in one place and the rain doesn't rain only on one person's rooftop. The greater the day, the greater the sun.